Sky Above,
Earth Below

Sky Above,
Earth Below

Spiritual Practice in Nature

John P. Milton

SENTIENT PUBLICATIONS, LLC

First Sentient Publications edition, 2006

Grateful acknowledgment is made to Sounds True, Boulder, Colorado, for permission to reproduce photographs from their audiotape set, *Sky Above, Earth Below*.

A paperback original

Cover design by Kim Johansen, Black Dog Design
Book design by Nicholas Cummings

Library of Congress Cataloging-in-Publication Data

Milton, John P.
  Sky above, earth below : spiritual practice in nature / by John P. Milton.-- 1st Sentient Publications ed.
    p. cm.
  ISBN 1-59181-028-0
  1. Nature--Religious aspects. 2. Spiritual life. I. Title.
BL435.M55 2004
202'.4--dc22

                                    2004012508

Printed in the United States of America

10 9 8 7 6 5 4 3 2 1

SENTIENT PUBLICATIONS
A Limited Liability Company
1113 Spruce St.
Boulder, CO 80302
www.sentientpublications.com

Contents

Presence

Cultivating Universal Energy

Contents

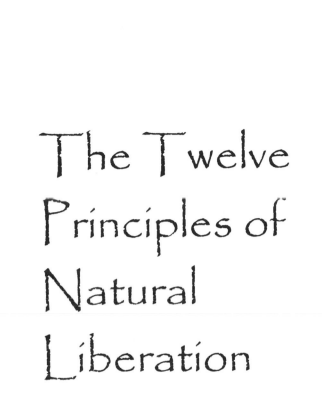

The Twelve Principles of Natural Liberation

IN AN ERA LONG BEFORE INDOOR CHURCHES and temples, people communed directly with sacred Spirit out upon the body of the Earth, embraced by the vastness of the sky above and the loving ground of the Earth below. Nature was experienced as a flowing creation of the Divine—a sanctuary of the wild where one could recognize life's sacredness without the interpretations of intermediaries. Earth was part of the physical form of Great Spirit; the sky mirrored the infinite immensity of the formless Being that birthed and held all creation.

The mystery of being in human form was explored through ancient shamanic practices by intimately working with all living beings and the sacred elements of Nature. In those times it was not uncommon for people to take extended solitary wilderness retreats and vision quests in forests, mountains, and deserts, where they opened to profound levels of spiritual realization. Animals, birds, and trees were seen as part of one's intimate family, and during vision quests were often viewed as great teachers for people. Because of this sacred view, all life was experienced as a whole—no separation of the sacred and the mundane, no arbitrary or harsh division between Spirit and matter. Mother Earth, Gaia, was the temple, the shrine, and the altar. She was the threshold to direct realization of the Great Nature that holds us all.

We, and our early human ancestors, have coevolved with Gaia through countless changes and migrations over millions of years. During that time, in a process of continual interaction with Nature and Earth, our physical, energetic, emotional, mental, and spiritual natures took form. Inner and outer nature coevolved together as part of a seamless web of life. This is why many of us feel so at home praying, meditating, and doing ceremony in wild Nature. Such natural ways of spiritual cultivation go back at least fifty thousand years and almost certainly more, in contrast to modern historical lineages and religious institutions that reach back six thousand years or less.

Today, our modern world is filled with high-tech wonders. Our urban and suburban existence surrounds us with crowded, artificial environments of plastic, steel, concrete, and glass. Environmental toxins, high-stress lifestyles, devitalized food, loud noise, unnatural electromagnetic fields, and microwave radiation assail our cells and sensibilities. Volatile chemical compounds often saturate our homes, offices, and communities. All these changes impose unique forms of anxiety, tension, and stress on us. They are destabilizing environments that are biologically quite new to humans. Our minds, emotions, and bodies are often unable to cope with these radically new artificial stresses. Consequently, rates of cancer, heart disease, obesity, emotional suffering, and psychological breakdown have spread rapidly along with the mushrooming worldwide impact of modern technology and ways of life.

When we leave these tensions for a while to cultivate our natural wholeness in the wild, we are renewed with the fresh vitality and spirit of Nature. New pathways open for living in harmony with our communities and the Earth. We discover deep inspiration to help transform our lifestyles and our culture toward harmony and balance.

Sky Above, Earth Below: Spiritual Practice in Nature distills the essence of many Earth-connected traditions that lead to realization of Source and to loving communion with Gaia and all living beings. Exposure to these traditions has opened, and continues to open, pathways leading from outer Nature into the essence of the deepest Source awareness within us. To assist contemporary cultures in walking the same path as the ancient wisdom cultures, I have distilled a series of twelve central principles and their associated practices for spiritual cultivation.

My "Twelve Principles of Natural Liberation" were essentialized over the past fifty years from personal training with many fine teachers, as well as from completing numerous meditation retreats, Sacred Passages, and vision quests in the wilderness. Great gifts of insight also came from living in some of Earth's wildest places, from residing in a number of her most sacred sites, and from working on many expeditions and environmental projects. Dwelling in remote cultures quite alien to modern times opened my view of what immense possibilities we carry as human beings; many of these cultures initiated me into the deeper shamanic view of what it means to be human. All of this experience has contributed greatly to defining the twelve principles. Even though many of my own teachers have been extraordinary in their teaching and transmission abilities, my own ability to receive and contain these teachings has often been limited. Therefore, I take complete responsibility for any errors or omissions in the creation of these twelve principles.

Although some of these sacred principles are clarified superbly by some of my teachers and mentors from differing traditions, in the end it was my hope to bring these core concepts together and essentialize them to show the common spiritual heart beating within most of the world's lineages. Once we can begin to see the common threads running through the matrix of this planet's human religions, then we can loosen the fixation on our own path as the only true path. We will no longer abuse or kill others if they refuse to join our creed; we will stop breeding intolerance towards those who have other religious forms, other symbols, other ways. Instead, these twelve principles may begin to show us how much we share in common with other traditions; as this unfolds, our self-righteous fundamentalism will wane. We may begin to honor the incredible diversity of how Spirit elucidates a particular principle, and even learn from this rich tapestry of expression.

Once I have introduced the twelve principles, this book will then focus on the core six principles of the twelve; these basic six principles represent an even more condensed form of the spiritual path. Throughout, I will also be emphasizing Nature, body, perception, cosmos, and Mother Earth as the most ancient and truest temples. We will also explore the depths of the innermost temple—the luminous, spacious shrine of Source that radiates from the living heart of all species and Gaia herself.

The Twelve Principles of Natural Liberation

As was mentioned above, the conception of the twelve principles presented here involved many years of study, deep training, and spiritual cultivation in some of the world's most profoundly enlightening, Earth-connected traditions. Starting in the 1950s, a variety of Nature-honoring, liberating lineages was an important

focus for my own training. Specifically, this training has emphasized Zen, Mahayana and Vajrayana Buddhism, Taoism, T'ai Chi
and Qi Gong, Dzogchen, Hindu and Buddhist Tantra, Vedanta,
and several shamanic paths. Also tremendously inspiring to me
have been the life and teachings of Henry David Thoreau and John
Muir, as well as the science of ecology. These twelve principles are
also a culmination of many years (starting in 1945) of solo immersion, vision quest, and spiritual practice in the wilderness. Out of
all this background came the essentialization of these principles.
For me, these sacred principles represent the common heart
essence of the world's liberating, Earth-honoring lineages.

My early solo vision quests started at age seven in New
Hampshire's White Mountains. I continued doing vision quests
two to four times a year into my teens and since then have continued with at least several quests each year throughout life. By the
mid-teens, my first month-long vision quest unfolded in
Washington State's Olympic Mountains. (Some of this Olympic
Mountain experience is shared later in this chapter.) All this early
wilderness solo experience profoundly transformed my view of
self, of humanity, and of all life. These transformations led, in my
early teens, to inviting young friends to do vision quests with me
in adjoining solo camps. I quickly discovered that some form of
preparatory training was important, even necessary, for the deepening and full fruition of their experience. I began to provide simple meditative training based on zazen practice outdoors in the
1950s, as well as on a number of practices that came directly as
gifts from Spirit. Most of these innovative practices had to do with
meditating outside on the fields of perception, and with unifying
oneself and Nature through sight, sound, touch, smell, taste,
movement, emotion, and thought.

As my formal training in zazen and Taoism deepened from
the late 1950s into the sixties and seventies, more inspiration to
serve others naturally arose. I continued to evolve and integrate
meditative and energy cultivation practices in Nature with the

vision questing process. This combination continues today as the basis for the twelve-day Sacred Passage Program, the Intermediate Awareness Training and 28 Day Solo, the four-year Advanced Awareness Training, the GaiaFlow system of movement, and the establishment of The Way of Nature, a fellowship of like-minded souls.

Beginning in the 1970s, I began to provide a more comprehensive training, which I came to call the Awareness Training, for those doing Sacred Passage trainings and solos with me. Many of my students came from extraordinarily diverse backgrounds and cultures. Because of this great diversity, I began to see the value of essentializing much of what I had learned into simple, direct teachings that could speak to a common heart within all people. This was the beginning of essentializing the twelve principles of natural liberation. At first they grew slowly. I recall that relaxation and presence were the first two that formed the core of the Awareness Training teachings. Since then, the principles have grown organically into the current twelve principles used today.

To build a strong foundation for the cultivation and realization of each principle, over decades I have integrated hundreds of practices into The Way of Nature's Awareness Training. Each principle now has a wide variety of practices to help support your realization of its essence. Every practice in this extensive practice array serves to cultivate the truth of each principle within. Since we are all diverse and unique in our makeup, this practice diversity helps fine-tune inner cultivation in a fashion that can be uniquely appropriate for each individual. A particular practice series that might be excellent for one person might be inappropriate for another. However, the help of a skilled guide or teacher is usually vital in helping select, teach, apply, and evolve a student's practice series. This guidance is important because we are often most blind to those areas where we need the most help. Our deepest blockages are often the most difficult for us to see. Here, a good teacher can be a godsend.

Most of these ways of cultivation have been drawn from traditional systems that have a proven track record, such as Buddhist and Taoist meditation, Tibetan shamanism, Chinese Qi Gong and T'ai Chi, Yoga, Indian Advaita Vedanta, and Dzogchen. In some cases, I or some of my senior students have created entirely new practices to help further spiritual realization. Currently, a body of over eight hundred practices supports deep cultivation, incorporation, and realization of all the twelve principles.

These principles are presented here in a progressive sequence of inner growth true for most people. For example, hearing the first principle—the interconnected and continually changing nature of all form arising and dissolving from primal Source—lays the proper foundation for engaging the second principle, our personal commitment to realizing this truth by accomplishing liberation. Spiritual commitment to liberation is vital for us to enter and progress along the path; spiritual liberation is also essential if we are to be truly helpful to all living beings. Yet the third principle, relaxation, is where most of us must actually begin to cultivate our inner exploration. If we are filled with bodily, emotional, and mental contractions, there is little room for meditation practice, much less for the unbounded openness of real spiritual insight. Releasing our contractedness lays the proper foundation for liberating our distractedness. Our distracted lives begin to naturally simplify by realizing the power of presence. This fourth principle, presence, is the necessary companion for relaxation. Pure presence in itself *is* the awakened view. Without the union of relaxation and presence, the essential qualities of alert, yet open and relaxed awareness cannot be realized. All the principles build on each other in this way.

Nevertheless, this sequential unfolding from the first to the last principle is not a hard and fast rule. The twelve principles ultimately are recognized as a multifaceted matrix, where one can enter from many doorways, depending upon our unique situation.

Taken together, these twelve principles and their associated practices form an all-denominational body of distinctive teachings that form the heart essence of The Way of Nature path.

Each principle represents a key seed to the opening of spiritual awakening common to each of the great liberating traditions—yet in The Way of Nature the true commitment is to direct spiritual illumination, rather than emphasis on the outer forms and symbols of a specific lineage or religion. It is my hope that the illumination of these twelve collective principles will help those of you practicing a particular religion. You can look forward to experiencing the fundamental nature of your path more clearly and to developing great respect for all the other paths that share these same universal principles. For those of you searching for a direct path to the sacred, these teachings are offered in the hope they will be helpful on your journey into the boundless.

A concise summary of the twelve principles for natural liberation follows:

1. The fundamental truth: All forms are interconnected, constantly change, and continuously arise from and return to primordial Source.

    All material forms and all energetic, perceptual, sensate, emotional, and thought forms are totally interconnected and interdependent. Also, all these forms, including the sense of individual self, are constantly changing and transforming. Fundamentally, all forms are in a continuous process of arising from, manifesting within, and dissolving back into primordial, essentially formless, Source awareness. At a deep level, all forms are transient and empty of permanent being. At the deepest level all forms, including ourselves, are a magical display of the boundless, formless Source that is our true essence. We have the choice of either resisting this fundamental truth, and suffering; or surrendering into this truth—and dancing in the flow.

2. Commit yourself completely to liberation in this lifetime.

I personally recommend that you commit yourself, one hundred percent, to complete liberation, the enlightened realization of fundamental truth, in this lifetime. Further, this principle recommends you dedicate all the fruits of your life and path to the greatest possible benefit and service for all beings.

3. Relax and surrender to life.

Deeply relax and profoundly surrender. To begin, first locate where you still hold contractions and tensions in your body, emotions, and mind. Then learn to decontract and relax your body, your emotions, your energy, your thoughts, and mind. Let go of old ideas, judgments, emotions, and structures; your own expectations; your need for approval or acceptance; and your idea of progress. Over time, replace your old habitual patterns of fear and automatic contraction to life with new, helpful habits of meeting life with openness and letting go. As you deepen yet further, come to completely trust your unfolding life. Trust yourself to unwind and empty completely and remain open to now. Ultimately, your deepening trust brings you to the ultimate level of this principle: surrender. In this most advanced stage, even the effort to let go and trust is released as you surrender completely to the flow of life's forms; your being effortlessly anchors in the stability of timeless presence.

4. Remain in now.

Become aware of your distractions. If need be, even meditate single-mindedly on the flow of your inner and outer distractions. Be patient. Over time, as you meditate regularly, the flow of distractions should begin to slow, allowing present-centered awareness to rise. Remain in that pure presence. Give more and more precise, clear attention to the now and here—meditate on the exact instant of the present moment and the surroundings—as you directly experience them. Release distractions even more deeply; stay with present perception, emotion, or thought as it arises, rather than withdrawing to the past or leaping ahead to the future. Refine nowness. Be precisely where you are. In fact, come to realize that being precisely where you are *is* the fundamental, inevitable truth. As gaps naturally appear between thoughts, as open spaces arise between emotions, rest in the gap. Let the clarity of your pure awareness settle naturally in itself. Enjoy the bliss of nowness.

5. Cultivate union with universal energy

As you relax, old bodily, emotional, energetic, and mental blockages are released, freeing up bound life force (which is called *chi* or *qi* by the Chinese—both are pronounced "CHEE"). When you combine present-centered awareness with relaxation, you can deepen the journey of unblocking your inner energy. Gently bring your awareness into deeper and deeper levels of body, emotions, and mind. Wherever inner obscurations are discovered, relax and intend to release them. Feel your life force liberated as you refine relaxation and presence within.

The union of relaxation and presence leads to natural cultivation of your life force. Remember that your mind's intent leads the qi. Combine this firm, yet gentle intent to clarify and gather life force with energy-cultivating postures and forms. Unify relaxation, presence, and intent. Find a peaceful, natural place outdoors where the energy is clear and renewing. With some practice, you should be able to feel this regenerating quality directly. Morning is the ideal time to absorb clear, fresh qi from Nature. Be totally present with the clear, relaxed intention to receive Nature's gifts of life force. Spend some quality time at a special place for you in Nature—each morning practicing Qi Gong or another energy cultivation discipline to purify, gather and refine your qi. Then absorb the healing energy of Nature through intention, presence, and relaxation.

Late afternoon and evening are good times to release blockages. At the close of your day, take some additional time to do energy practices that help clear away accumulated blockages and obscurations. Before and after your inner cultivation, morning and evening, give thanks for the gifts of healing qi from the plants, from the stones, from the elements, from the Sun and Moon and from Mother Earth.

For the rest of your waking hours, as you move through your daily challenges, learn to spontaneously purify blockages in your energy body with these developing skills of unified relaxation, presence, and intent. Learn to renew your life force in the midst of daily activity. Without union with universal energy there can be no true transformation. The cultivation methods we teach and utilize in The Way of Nature include Qi Gong, Taoist meditation, T'ai Chi, Yoga, Dzogchen energy cultivation work, and specific shamanic energy practices to work directly with Nature, the cosmos, and the elements. Many of these are unified in our unique system of naturally liberating movement, GaiaFlow.

6. Go with the universal flow.

Ultimately, over a lifetime of practice, you may realize true energy mastery: the ability to flow in complete union with universal energy, no matter what may be happening externally. Here the path of liberation through energy cultivation reaches its completion. At this point, the need for formal energy practices falls away. This principle is included here as a reminder that ultimately even attachment to powerful energy cultivating practices, as in Taoism, Tantra, and Dzogchen, are released. At this stage of liberation through energy cultivation, the flow of natural movement and stillness effortlessly express the creative Source. One's experience of the creative dance of form and energy is pure bliss manifesting in the field of Source awareness.

7. Rest in the radiance of your open heart.

    Relaxation and presence unify within to help unblock and cultivate the radiant life force. You realize and experience this radiance as pure, unconditional love. There are no preconditions for this experience, which naturally arises as the direct innermost quality of relaxed, present, liberated energy. Through the natural deepening of this openhearted radiance, the separation between self and other gradually dissolves.

8. Active compassion arises naturally out of unconditional love.

    The natural activity of open, unconditioned love is compassionate action. This expressive kindness spontaneously arises, moment by moment from your heart essence. Your compassionate activity can manifest through inner practices like Tonglen, or through outer service in eliminating suffering and in bringing peace and happiness to all living beings. This opening of the heart into active compassion arises naturally from the inner unfolding of principles one through seven.

9. Cut through to clarity.

    Cut through to the clarity, spaciousness, and luminosity of pure Source awareness. In some cases, this cutting through occurs with the help of your human teacher; in other cases it may arise through the grace of the Great Mystery. Such a cutting through event may be powerful, like a thunderbolt; or it may be very subtle, like the sound of a leaf falling to touch the

Earth. Powerful or subtle, it stops the world in an instant, and cuts through all distractions, contractions, attachments, and aversions—all obstacles—to the direct experience of Source. Inner obscurations, including attachment to the bliss of an open heart, are cut through in a moment, laying bare pristine awareness—the naked essence of Source.

10. Return to Source.

The ninth principle cracks through the ego's seed coat that has been blocking off Source. With dawning clear awareness, Source is realized as the underlying reality out of which all form, including you yourself, manifests. This primordial unconditioned is formless, yet gives birth to all form, holds all form, and is the ultimate receptacle for the dissolution of all form. Source has skylike unbounded spaciousness and clarity. Applied to an individual, Source is the most fundamental, simple, complete, and perfect actuality that is who we really are. Because no term can really describe it, I often simply point to it by calling it the Great Mystery.

It can be realized by following our perceptions back to primordial awareness—that pure consciousness within ourselves which is our deepest nature. When that essence is realized, one realizes it is indestructible. It is infinite and beyond all conventional measurements and descriptions. It was never born and never dies. The closer one approaches Source, the more synchronous events become. When Source is accessed, extraordinary creativity occurs. Most great inventions and breakthroughs have arisen through deep communion with Source.

11. Pure Source awareness is—remain in recognition.

Remain in continuous, complete, flowing recognition of Source awareness: the formless clear light—unborn, undying, and boundless. When one has mastered principles one through ten, one's path naturally culminates in remaining in Source awareness. Full commitment to the previous ten principles (and the practices that cultivate them) inevitably results in remaining in perfect, continuous recognition of Source. This is the natural condition of perfect liberation; all forms, inner and outer, are simply experienced as the natural display of Source's pure creativity.

12. Serve as a warrior of the open heart and liberated spirit.

This is a warrior-like principle. But the warriorship comes in the challenge of opening your deepest levels of living the twelve principles. Not just for yourself, but allowing them to flower into serving other humans, all species, and Gaia (Mother Earth) herself. Here you come back to the full embrace of the world, whatever your degree of accomplishment in integrating the previous eleven principles into your life and being. The key is to bring each of these principles into creative interaction with the challenges of everyday life. As you actively cultivate each principle, you dedicate your activity to the happiness and liberation of all those beings in your field of relationship.

For example, in applying the third principle, you not only relax contractedness in your own life, but you also seek to help others become more open, relaxed, and trusting. When relating to the eighth principle, you become a compassionate warrior of the open heart in active service for all life. Wherever possible, you bring loving, compassionate assistance to all living beings.

With the full application of the twelfth principle, ultimately all eleven previous principles are naturally unified and expressed in the moment-by-moment radiation of compassionate, liberated activity creatively arising from Source. All the principles become naturally unified; you dedicate yourself to compassionate support for all life in all aspects of normal existence—in your business, your civil, your ecological, and your personal lives.

The eleventh principle is clear, spontaneous recognition of Source in all circumstances. Source, the formless clear light of pure awareness, is itself the ultimate origin of all creativity. Out of your deepening communion with Source, continuously arise fresh, innovative ways to engage life. These new forms of creative response, when they are clearly recognized as arising from original primordial awareness, have the capacity to bring profoundly appropriate new means of healing, happiness, integration, and liberation for all our relations. The deeper One rests in formless Source, the vaster the creative upwelling of freshly evolved forms—forms in the service of the whole and all its parts.

Embracing this pure creative insight through trust and loving, liberated action is the heart path of the compassionate warrior.

13. Don't take all these twelve principles too seriously.

- Don't become attached to all of these principles.

- Laugh.

- Celebrate life's gift.

- Enjoy coyote's howl.

The Six Core Principles of Natural Liberation

The following chapters will introduce to you six core principles of spiritual cultivation. Essentialized from my twelve principles briefly outlined above, the following six principles represent the central teachings in this book. These six core principles of natural liberation include:

1. Relaxation

2. Presence

3. Cultivating universal energy

4. Opening the heart of unconditional love

5. Cutting through to clarity, luminosity, and spaciousness

6. Returning to Source

In order to ground your being and support the inner flowering of these core principles, this book offers many useful practices for you to cultivate in the days, weeks, and months ahead. For many who have studied with me over the years and applied these teachings to their lives, these principles and associated practices have provided profound transformation. The quality of their relationships with others, their creativity, and their enjoyment of life have invariably been powerfully transformed. Almost all report a fresh and deeply renewed bond with Mother Earth. Many experience significant new insights, having touched into the clear, limitless, formless awareness of their essence. Over a longer time of practice and application, some people tell of going through a complete transformation of their being, an all-embracing inner rebirth.

No Separation Between Spirit and Nature

When I first began going into wild Nature, I was quite young. My grandparents had a wonderful organic farm on a small mountaintop in northern New Hampshire and, together with parents, sisters, brothers, aunts, uncles, and cousins, we all ran the farm together. Even before I could speak, I remember crawling through blueberry patches in the wild meadows on our hillsides. I quickly discovered Nature was filled with Spirit; I never saw any separation between Spirit and Nature. Much later I discovered our culture taught there was supposed to be some kind of separation—that God, Spirit, and Nature were supposed to be divided and different. However, at my early age it seemed absolutely obvious that the church of the Earth was the greatest church of all; that the temple of the forest was the supreme temple. When I went to the sanctuary of the mountain, I found Earth's natural altar—Great Spirit's real shrine. Years later I discovered that this path of going into Nature, bonding deeply with it, and seeing Spirit within Nature—God, Goddess, and Great Spirit—was humanity's most ancient, most primordial path of spiritual cultivation and realization.

As a young boy, I went into buildings called churches and temples. Yes, there was sometimes a feeling of the sacred there, but it seemed very limited, constrained, and artificial compared to the natural communion and insights that I was receiving out in the wild.

Alone in the Temple of the Woods

When I was seven years old, I had a very natural feeling of wanting to embrace Nature. A passionate feeling for Mother Earth arose; I wanted to spend all my time with her. I implored my parents and grandparents for time to be alone, all one, in the wilderness forests and granite mountains of northern New Hampshire's White Mountains. That year, 1945, my mother and grandfather helped put me out on my first vision quest in those mountains.

A "vision quest" refers to embracing Nature and Spirit in a special way. To Native Americans a vision quest means surrendering to Nature and Spirit in a sacred way to deepen relationships with the mystery of life, the mystery of you, the mystery of Nature, the mystery of Great Spirit. A vision quest means praying for a vision of the truth of your life. At its deepest level, a vision quest means awakening to the view of all life and existence as sacred. If one is truly graced, then formless Source opens as the pristine foundation of all.

This first four-day, three-night solo in the wilderness was a sacred time of tremendous opening. I was absorbed into passionate fusion with Father Sky and Mother Earth, with sky above and Earth below. The fundamental unity of all people with Nature and Great Spirit was clear. Embraced by this union of Nature and universal Spirit; the universal heart opened completely in perfect integration. This early vision quest experience opened a profound path—a path that still spirals through my being.

This path of going alone into the woods, mountains, and swamps intensified because of a passion for Nature; it felt like the most natural thing to do. Every journey into the wild became an intense love affair with all life. The trees and birds, the flowers and mountains, the streams and rivers spoke clearly. The meaning behind the movements of birds and songs of animals was unmistakable. I could feel what the trees were feeling. There was no separation when the forests and I swayed in the breeze. My being could move like a bobcat or a bear through the forest. Nature taught this way; she taught through her presence and her love. She displayed the tremendous diversity in the way Nature is, and she clarified the underlying unity of Spirit that embraces all natural forms. I trusted that.

Over the years the mystery deepened. From the mid-1940s until now, I have been able to vision quest at least once a year, and often three or four times a year. As I entered the teens, these sacred solos grew longer and longer. In the mid-1950s, vision questing opened into a full month-long lunar cycle in the heart of the Olympic Mountains in Washington. By 1960, the process culminated in a three-month plunge into the largest and last unmapped, uncharted wilderness of the American Rockies: the Logan

Mountains of the upper Nahanni River watershed in arctic Canada's Northwest Territories. This wilderness solo at that time was an astonishing baptism into the mystery beyond naming and describing.

The Olympic Mountains

Washington's lofty Olympic Mountains loom large on the humid peninsula west of Seattle. These glacier-clad peaks, gleaming with snow and ice, rise above some of the most beautiful temperate rain forests in the world. I had longed to go there to do my first month-long vision quest. At age fifteen, with the help of father and grand-father, I was able to get a job as a very young salmon fisherman in southeast Alaska's panhandle region of wild islands, coasts, and secluded bays. In those days, Alaska had not become a state; it was still a U.S. territory. The fishing job there was not due to start until July, which gave all of June for the vision quest.

The Olympic Mountains form a great circular mass of sum-mits and ridges with deeply forested valleys radiating out from the core. At the heart of the mountains, my map disclosed a divide—the Low Divide—that connected one of the main northern valleys with one of the main southern drainages. I knew this was where I needed to vision quest. The north-south arrangement of the two valleys allowed a walk across the entire mountain range, from north to south, and made possible a vision quest in the heart of the mountains surrounding the Low Divide. The walk south through the temperate rain forest was a journey into a moss-draped heaven. The forest floor, tree trunks, and every limb were clothed in an extraordinary display of mosses and lichens of every conceivable shade of green.

Upon finishing the trek up to the Low Divide, I set up camp in an alpine meadow under a rising full moon. High summits nearby, clothed in snow and glacial ice, shone pale in the moonlight while I fell asleep that first evening. Strange sounds sometime around midnight brought a sudden awakening. All around arose the sounds of some gigantic animal moving around my tiny tent and occasionally brushing against it. As the crackling and snorting sounds amplified, visions arose of the biggest bear in the mountains preparing to invade the tent. A grizzly? Terror chilled the bones.

Somehow, enough courage came to open a crack in the tent door and peer cautiously outside. There in the moonlight was my huge fearsome beast—a whole herd of well over one hundred Olympic elk had meandered onto the divide and were now moving peacefully all around. Branches broke, twigs cracked, and gentle grunts accompanied their calm movement over the pass. In an instant, my fear exploded into bliss. That transformation triggered an opening of pure joy that lasted without a break for the next four weeks of the solo mountain passage. The sacred view opened in a close embrace.

That liberating time gave me a powerful vision, a view of how to bring the vision quest process into the heart of western culture. The vision made clear that these sacred solos had the power to be a profoundly enlightening seed. These seed openings could totally transform people's disharmony with all life and lead people's lives in new directions. These new directions would be founded on discovering a deep reunion with the Source of their being, and on opening a profound communion with Mother Earth. The vision shared that this process was the medicine Western culture needed to come back into balance and harmony with the Earth and all of Nature. The vision quest would become the ultimate remedy for a culture lost in the rape and plunder of Gaia. The wilderness solo would be part of an all-denominational, interfaith path that led directly back to the Great Mystery and the Source of all Creation.

Over the following few years, the truth of this early vision became clearer and clearer. Realization deepened that the vision quest (or Sacred Passage) path could be immensely helpful to many people. It also became clear that our culture was terrifically out of balance with the Earth—that, as humans, we had lost the ability to live and grow in harmony with the Earth and her life-renewing principles. Also, the liberation that can arise directly and naturally from time alone in Nature, was coming to be an extremely rare realization for the great majority of people from planet Earth's increasingly urbanized and technologized cultures. The naturalness of life was somehow vanishing, particularly for modern people. A dangerous separation was growing apparent between human beings and the rest of Nature. Many persons, particularly those who spent most of their lives living in cities, were both isolated and alienated from the natural world. Urban dwellers, those separated from Nature and from the wild, rarely felt the extraordinary essence of the great being goddess Gaia, Mother Earth.

Sharing the Adventure with Others

In my early teens (1951–53), I began to share vision quests with other people. Initially, guiding focused on young friends eager to explore this kind of engagement with Nature. All of us were close in age. Going into solo camps to do the vision quest, we would support each other by bringing in gear together and establishing solo checkpoints. Beforehand, we would share what we felt about, or had learned from, Nature and Great Spirit. We did this in a simple way—nothing complicated. After three to five nights of solo, we would come back together and reveal some of the openings and experiences that we'd had. Usually we were amazed at the depth of our experiences. Even though in separate camps, we noticed many similar experiences occurred. One of the most common results, no matter what our background, was a shared opening of great love and appreciation for Nature.

Dropping the Illusions of City Comfort

By the mid-1950s, I began offering vision quests to people from a few cities near my family's winter home in New Jersey. In the beginning, some of these folks were a bit frightened and unsure of themselves. A number of them had never left New York City, Newark, Jersey City, or Hoboken. However, for those who joined in, the pull to experience the essence of themselves and the ancient truths of Nature and Spirit was more powerful.

As we went out into the wild, I found that there were additional supportive ways to help people bond with Nature and touch their soul. Early work was on sharing simple meditation practices—ways to meditate with Nature as a partner—and developing tracking and other Earth observation skills. By 1955, I was also beginning to practice zazen and Taoist meditation outdoors; this background helped me pass along basic skills to cultivate clear awareness and to work with transforming the strong emotions that often would come up. All this helped intensify spiritual unfolding in Nature. Sharing these early teachings also served to help crystallize what later became the more formal Awareness Training and Sacred Passage processes.

By my late teens, it became clear that many of those guided and prepared for vision quests were able to venture into Nature with less fear. They were able to experience deep connections and insights into the wild, their own spirit, and Great Nature—even though many had spent their whole lives living in cities. Many of them had no formal spiritual or meditative practice, yet most immediately sensed a natural kinship with the wild.

The veneer of civilization is not so deep. For nearly all people, the thin veil of culture usually begins to dissolve in just a few days of entering a vision quest or Sacred Passage solo. The artificial begins to be replaced by the genuine; the reality of inner and outer nature arises. The illusion of separation from Earth diminishes and is replaced by the awesome beauty, vitality, and wild energy of

Great Nature. One's inner being dances in harmony with Nature and Great Spirit's display.

Integrated Teachings

Also in the 1950s, I began to practice Zen meditation and Qi Gong with a fine teacher who had just come from Japan. From the mid-1960s and on through the 1970s, this inner work expanded with the study of T'ai Chi Ch'uan and some of the Taoist meditative practices from China with a variety of other fine teachers. In addition, from 1967 through the 1980s, my study deepened in Nepal and India with some extraordinary masters from the Hindu Tantric and Vedantic traditions, as well as from several Vipassana and Tibetan Buddhist lineages. All this training began to naturally integrate with the vision quest background to produce an early form of the Awareness Training and the twelve principles, which are now the vital heart of the vision quest process I have since developed. This body of work and program offering is now called Sacred Passage, which is the lead program for The Way of Nature Fellowship. The fellowship was founded in the 1980s to provide a broader vehicle for this interfaith, Earth-centered spiritual process. Today the heart essence of The Way of Nature includes the Awareness Training, the twelve principles, a variety of wilderness solos from three to one hundred and eight days' duration, the classical Native American vision quest, and a liberating, Gaia-embracing spirituality.

Many teachings also come from spontaneous insights received during years of deep immersion in Great Nature. Unifying these teachings with the inspiring realizations of the great Earth-connected and liberating traditions conveys tremendous benefit, both to me and to all the other friends and students who share in these insights and practices. Nature in the pristine wilderness, and Great Spirit moving through Nature, have always been the most profound teachers.

It is a delight to be able to share these same teachings with you now. Over the years, I've focused on distilling all the Awareness Training teachings and practices into the twelve principles of natural liberation summarized earlier. These principles can help move you very deeply into Source awareness and the union of inner and outer nature. These twelve principles have been further condensed into this text's core six principles for clearer understanding and cultivation. These are the six core principles of natural liberation. As one follows The Way of Nature path, these principles are normally experienced in regular progression from first to final principle shared here. However, as a spiritual path, these principles also operate as a nonlinear matrix.

Again, these six core principles of natural liberation are:

1. *Relax.* You open the path by releasing all forms of contraction, tension, blockage, and holding on to past, present, and future. This principle helps you to be truly open to what is there, within yourself and within Nature. Ultimately, it is experienced as a complete surrender into the truth of here and now.

2. *Be present.* Once you have begun to clear away your tensions and blockages, the possibility of realizing presence naturally arises. This principle allows you to connect precisely with whatever is appearing, within and without. All distractions dissolve in the only time there is: now.

3. *Cultivate universal energy (i.e., life force, prana, or qi).* Cultivation of universal energy gives you the vitality to move deeper and deeper on the spiritual path. The union of presence and relaxation, then combined with the power of intent, is the key to opening greater vitality. Amplified life force helps wake you up and helps clear away old blockages. As pure universal

energy, its main experiential quality is unqualified loving-kindness.

4. *Open the heart in unconditional love.* Supported by your cultivation of relaxation, presence, and universal energy, your heart begins to open into unconditional love. Initially, this loving energy permeates your being with the joy and bliss of an opening heart. You discover compassionate activity is the natural expression of an unconditionally loving heart.

5. *Cut through to clarity, spaciousness, and luminosity.* This principle includes learning to take advantage of times when surprising and cutting-through experiences happen. Also, this cutting through includes slicing through the tendency to stay in the bliss rather than continue on the way to full liberation. In some traditions, this cutting through has been called "stopping the world." It could also be called "severing the discursive mind at its root." Pure primordial awareness, sheer Source, arises, at least for a moment. The experience of this principle opens the wisdom of tremendous spaciousness and clarity on the spiritual path.

6. *Return to Source.* At the start of this profound principle, having at least once recognized Source, you continue cultivating inner and outer nature to rediscover deepest Source within. Eventually, one apprehends the subtle dualism of seeker and sought, and is able to truly surrender in profound presence. Naked essence is realized. Ultimately, all contrived and artificial attempts to recognize one's fundamental nature are released. One flows in spontaneous self-liberation of all that arises.

As we delve deeply into each of these six principles in the following chapters, you will find a number of practices that will help you to cultivate each principle at a profound level. You will discover how to cultivate these sacred principles and practices in the wild. These processes will help you open the essence of each principle in yourself. You will blossom as an integrated being. Inner tranquility, peace, and harmony will flower. The return to Source clarifies.

Relaxation

THE JOURNEY WE ARE ABOUT TO BEGIN will take us into the immensity of the wild—the vastness of Nature in its pure and primordial state. This is a journey that will bring Nature into your heart. Deep relaxation awakens the tranquil heart of spiritual cultivation in Nature. As you refine both inner and outer nature, you will begin to experience them in natural union. Over time, you may even gain glimpses of that Great Nature that holds you and all Nature's forms.

Most of us carry numerous contractions and distractions into the flow of our daily lives. These contractions act as barriers or shields that prevent us from directly experiencing life's fullness. They block us from having a clear experience of Nature's sweeping array of sights, sounds, tastes, smells, and shades of touch. If you are contracted, often you are obstructed from your true feelings and thoughts about inner and outer nature as well. These same blockages commonly interfere with the natural flow of energy through your body, energetic channels, meridians, and chakras. Unattended, these blockages can lead to lowered vitality, an impoverished quality of life, and illnesses of many kinds.

Nature is also an extraordinary healer. If you simply give her a chance by spending a little time letting her embrace you, she will begin to merge with your energy, emotions, and thoughts. She will begin to heal many of the anxieties that you carry. Nature is a very powerful healer.

Our contractions have many sources, but one of their most common origins arises from strong negative emotions such as fear, anger, sadness, anxiety, and worry. A powerful way to transform these blockages is simply to practice relaxation and letting go in situations that would normally contract us. But before we can do this, we must first learn how to relax. Developing the skills of relaxation require the following: first, good instruction in helping you discover where your blockages are; second, learning the techniques of relaxation from a good teacher; third, locating a supportive environment, ideally one in Nature, where you can formally practice relaxation regularly; and fourth, cultivating relaxation at least once or twice a day.

In undertaking all this, be kind and patient with yourself. Most of us have built up powerfully domineering forms of tension, blockage, and contractedness over many years. Since our culture provides few opportunities to learn, much less master relaxation, most of us have a lot of letting go to accomplish. Fortunately, formal relaxation meditation practice done regularly can work miracles over time. The key is patient, persistent daily cultivation of this quality. Once you have begun to learn how to relax in this way, you can begin to cultivate relaxation in situations that formerly would have made you tense.

Cultivating relaxation in Nature, if you are careful to select a supportive time and place outdoors, can work magic in developing your ability to let go. Our cells, our DNA, our tissues and organs, our whole bodies, our energy, our diverse emotions, and our mind, all have coevolved with Nature and Gaia over billions of years. Yet, consider the massive experiment that modern society is conducting on us and on all natural systems, with unknown results.

Modern, high-tech urban culture is an extremely recent development in the history of our species. We have had little time biologically to adapt to contemporary fast-paced, crowded urban lifestyles. For example, the increased tension and contraction from our addiction to high-speed living is radical. Our biology is now bombarded with unfamiliar chemicals that are ingested, inhaled, and in contact with the skin. Our energy fields now interact with microwaves, electromagnetic waves, and magnetic fields completely novel to our organisms. Instead of walking, we are whisked about by cars and airplanes. Instead of being surrounded by earth, wood, stone, natural water, and uncontaminated sky, we now live within concentric cocoons of synthetic materials, concrete, steel, plastic, polluted water, and filthy air.

Many of our contemporary tensions and contractions are due to this onslaught of harsh artificial elements in our modern world. Particularly in large cities and urban areas, we are surrounded with crime and people going through all kinds of intense stress. These factors make it extremely difficult to move into an internal state of natural trust and letting go.

Contrast this with the ancient rhythms that once bonded human nature and universal Nature. The cycles of the Moon were reflected in female menstruation and in people rising to the Sun and sleeping after sunset. They ate directly from Nature with no intermediaries. They had direct, daily contact with Earth and Earth's natural geomagnetic fields underfoot. And they had close contact with the natural diversity and organic harmony of whole living ecosystems as their true home. Studies of aboriginal hunting and gathering cultures show only two to three hours a day were required to provide food, shelter, clothing, and other basics; the remaining time was free for ceremony, play, music, dance, other arts, meditation, and lovemaking. Contrast that with how many hours we invest today in taking care of modern basics.

When we return to Nature in her more ancient, pristine ecosystems—Nature as Gaia—we also return to an intricate web of environmental relationships that our organisms coevolved with over millions of years. Once we return to that natural organic affiliation, our cells, tissues, and whole organism begin to relax back into an ancient and deeply familiar relationship. The veneer of artificial contemporary living is quickly replaced by a great sense of relief and release. Our biology sings.

So, first, begin to explore your true nature *in Nature*, and when you start down the liberating path with this first powerful principle of mastering relaxation, be sure to start with cultivating it outside in a natural place. If you are fortunate enough to be near true wilderness or a wild place, count your blessings and go there to practice. If you are even luckier, you may be near one of the ancient sacred sites utilized by peoples since before time was measured. If so, go there in humility and ask for its blessing for your practice. Be sure to dedicate all the positive results of your cultivation time to the happiness and liberation of all beings, especially those caught by the yoke of modern living. Whatever natural area you go to, take whatever time is workable for you and start. It may be for only an hour or two, or perhaps you will be graced enough to do a full-fledged Sacred Passage or vision quest. The main thing is this: With whatever time you have available, go into Nature and start cultivating relaxation there.

If, because of weather or other circumstances, you are unable to practice outside, you can still do this cultivation work indoors, using the scanning meditation shared later in this text. You can still follow the spirit of these practices by doing them in an indoor garden, near an altar, or in a place in your dwelling that has a natural and sacred feel.

Once you are back in a natural place, it is essential to learn how to let go of the city anxieties and blockages you have brought into the wild. As long as those blockages are there, it will be difficult for you to let go and be open to what Nature has to offer. So when you are learning how to do spiritual practice in the wild, it is extremely important that you start with learning how to relax. I usually say to my students that the first issue to be faced in wilderness cultivation is learning how to release the contractions that they bring to Nature. As long as you have contractions within yourself, you have no space for Nature to begin to connect with you. You have no room to make a connection with either inner or outer nature.

Once you give her the chance, Nature can provide a wonderful support for learning relaxation. Perhaps you recall relaxing in a warm spring meadow where Mother Earth absorbed your tensions; or resting in the cool, fresh shade of a forest that calmed emotional anxiety; or unwinding on a mountain, where the spacious view helped all your troubles dissolve in the vastness of the sky. However Nature may support you, developing the skill of relaxation is a supremely valuable art in the stressful world of modern life.

Noticing Tension

The process of relaxation unfolds in stages. You might think that relaxation comes naturally, but actually relaxation requires cultivation and regular, persistent attention. In the beginning, you must first become aware that you are contracted. Discovering and paying attention to these contractions is the first step to relaxation (See the relaxation exercises at the end of this chapter for ideas about how to locate tension in your body.) You can carry tight muscles and other blockages in your body for years and not be aware of these tightenings, except that they sometimes feel a little painful. Noticing the when and where of your contractions is how you begin to face the truth that holding your inner blockages prevents you from going deeper into your true nature.

Relaxing with the Wind

An example of how humans commonly contract in Nature is illustrated by our physical response to a cool wind. When you contract against the wind, you may think to yourself, *I'm cold.* After that, your contracting thought guides your whole body to constrict further, which actually makes you feel even colder.

The next time you feel a cool wind, try relaxing into the feel of the breeze blowing over your skin without contracting your body. Simply surrender into the sensation without naming or judging it. You may notice that you feel a beautiful tingling and openness to the flow of energy rather than an increased constriction and coldness.

De-Contracting

Once you have addressed the contractions you hold, the next stage of relaxation is de-contraction. If you have not first discovered where you are holding anxiety and tension, then not much progress can be made because those tensions and anxieties are invisible to you. Learning how to master this process of opening to de-contraction is similar to gradually letting go and opening a fiercely clenched fist.

After you become aware of these constrictions and tensions in yourself, one of the best things you can do is go into a wild place to focus on de-contraction (see relaxation exercises at the end of this chapter). Go to an inspirational place in Nature and allow her healing energy to move into you and join with you to help the natural process of relaxation and opening.

Establishing Relationship

Initially, you may not be fully comfortable with being able to relax in Nature. You may encounter an unfamiliar world. It may be magical and mysterious, but it also may be somewhat scary or threatening, especially if you have not spent a lot of time in the wild. If that is the case, give yourself some time to adjust and be gentle with yourself. As you are starting on this path into the wild, it is good to go out into Nature alone, in a simple and safe way. Make a connection with Nature wherever you feel comfortable, and in a way that you feel protected and nurtured. You do not have to start with a vision quest in the wild forests of northern New Hampshire. Perhaps a familiar neighborhood natural area would be a better place to start. Move into Nature at a pace that does not push you to an extreme.

Also, begin the journey of natural relaxation slowly. At first, spend a little time each day in your local park or a natural place. After your practice deepens, consider going to a wilder place for a longer period of cultivation, possibly a whole day or a full weekend. As long as you spend some time each day practicing, over time you will definitely notice a shift, an opening, a releasing.

From earliest time, all the paths of spiritual practice in the wild have been based upon deepening relationships. Move toward those things that naturally draw you. Without establishing a relationship with all the incredible beings of Nature, there is really no way for human beings to open the path of the wild.

Just as in human relationships, it can be intimidating when you are first starting a relationship with other beings of Nature. You might not be quite sure how to behave. It is okay if you feel like that in the beginning of your association, as it basically shows that there is a powerful potential for something really magnificent to happen. Trust the process of cultivating a relationship with Nature. Your bond will open and flower in a way that will amaze you. It just needs time.

Letting Go, Deepening into Trust, and Surrender

Relaxation usually involves a progressive process, a series of natural stages. First, you discover where you are blocked and constricted. Next, you open into the mystery of learning how to reverse the contractions—how to de-contract. In the subsequent stage, you allow true relaxation to naturally arise. Next, the process of relaxation matures into a new pattern of letting go. Instead of building up layers of blockage and tension to shield you from change, you learn to consistently let go into the changes.

As you travel deeper into letting go, ultimately you arrive at the threshold of a core blockage—your fundamental mistrust and fear of life and death, your basic denial of now. The door that opens through this threshold is trust. In this case complete relaxation is necessary. Let go and trust the truth of your entire life situation, that which you comprehend and that which you cannot comprehend. When these first two stages of relaxation are mastered, letting go and deepening into trust, what arises is the first principle, surrender. In a very real sense, when surrender to the Great Mystery is realized, the path is completed simply through the full maturation of the principle of relaxation.

Summary Thoughts on Relaxation

At a young age I decided to spend time in Nature simply by walking, listening, being quiet, and relaxing. In Nature I learned how to let go of the accumulated tensions, stresses, and strains that many of us in modern culture carry with us every day.

My practice became one of simply quieting down, relaxing, and learning how to be in Nature in a way that was very open and spacious. In some ways this level of deep relaxation takes a little time and patience, but in other ways it can happen very quickly if you simply learn how to let go and deepen the process of release. This letting go of accumulated tension is most important when we are beginning to cultivate spiritual practice in Nature. Of all the tensions that plague our psyche, fear is the mother of most of them.

There are only a few things in Nature that can really harm a human being; fear itself is really the foremost danger. When you come to Nature with an attitude of trust, you will be received as a member of Gaia's family. With Mother Earth, you have the opportunity to really let go and trust in a way that you may have never done before. You can learn to open in a way that is totally new and fresh. If you come to Gaia with the view that Nature is sacred, then all of Gaia will respond in a sacred way.

A Note about the Exercises in this Book

At the end of each chapter, I have included various exercises to help you experience the embodiment of each principle. The explanations of these exercises are quite complete, with many details. To provide you maximum benefit, the value of repetition is emphasized. You can always simplify a practice to suit your needs. You can make them longer or shorter to accommodate your available time. Do not let the complexity of an exercise prevent you from trying it. If you feel the need to shorten or condense these practices, do so until you feel ready to take on the more comprehensive versions presented in this text. Please embrace them and make them your own. I designed these practices for you, so adapt the exercises in a way that is most workable.

I recommend you utilize a tape recording of the instructions for each exercise. All of these exercises are available on my *Sky Above, Earth Below* audiotape series offered by Sounds True in Boulder, Colorado. Sounds True has provided a wonderful service by making these practices available in a high-quality recorded format. The six-audiotape set includes a small book that features many of the same meditations. Another alternative is to make your own recording of the meditations. This will allow you to listen to your own voice guiding you through the details of each practice.

These practices were designed for regular, daily cultivation. Instead of looking on them as another obligation, experience them as I do, as the high point of your day. These processes will bring you release of anxiety, relaxation, vitality, inner spaciousness, and clarity. Realizing this, look forward to that time each day and week when you can cultivate them. Once you realize the inherent happiness these exercises can bring, there is no need to depend on always having a group or outer teacher there with you.

If you find it difficult to do all of these practices in one day, then rotate them throughout the week at your own pace. Be sure to spend some time contemplating the six core principles of natural liberation. This contemplation will greatly enhance the effectiveness of your spiritual cultivation.

The Source of Imbalance and Contractions in Our Society

Our species faces serious difficulties throughout the world. One of the reasons that we see so much human contractedness, separation, alienation, and anxiety is that we live out of balance with the natural environment. We no longer live in a world where everything is integrated, interconnected, balanced, and harmonious. Most of the time, Nature lives in a harmonious, integrated way. Even her catastrophic events, such as floods, lightning, hurricanes, volcanic eruptions, and the leap of a lioness on her prey, when seen in a broader view, are one with a harmonious, ecologically integrated Gaia. As I mentioned earlier, all the beings of Mother Earth have coevolved with each other in living, mutually interactive environments. All of these ecosystems, and the beings that live within them, have coevolved in a way that has produced extraordinary symbiosis, balance, integration, and harmony.

By contrast, our modern culture is still highly experimental. When humans stepped out of that natural world to create the artificially built environment, they began to lose their connection to the natural world. In a sense, they did step out of the Garden of Eden. We must be honest about this. We must face our shadow and honor the truth of our contractions and blockages. Due to this primordial separation with the natural world, you may be holding and suppressing anxieties and tensions that you are not even aware of. Your first step to uncover and acknowledge this disconnection, and the ancient angst that has arisen from this separation, is to begin to go into Nature on a regular basis.

By immersing in wild Nature—Nature that has not been heavily disturbed and damaged—you begin to tap back into the primal natural harmony that is your genetic inheritance. You return to a primordial church, an ancient natural temple that provides amazing healing power. The primeval energy and spirit of Nature provide your consciousness and your organic form with natural vitality and harmony of spirit that are not accessible in our urban centers.

The Integral Human

I have been fortunate to spend time with Taoist sages who are remarkable masters of harmony and balance. Nearly every one of them has spent long periods of time in wild Nature and surrendered to Great Nature, the unnamable Tao, as their primary teacher. One Taoist view that most impressed me was the way the sages described the fulfillment of the highest level of human potential and ability. They explained that becoming an integral one represents the greatest accomplishment a human can attain. An integral one is a human who has reached the full flowering of their potential and who lives in a completely integrated, essentialized state. All the elements, all the different aspects of the self are in complete harmony with the whole cosmos. The awareness rests in its free, unbounded, formless Source essence. All forms arise, display, and return to Source effortlessly, and yet, the Source remains unchanging.

Integration is characteristic of virtually everything in Nature. Integration is the way every form in Gaia functions when it rests in its primordial condition of interrelatedness. All beings in Nature carry this inner harmony. When you step forward into that world of the wild, into that world of the primal, you tap right back into your ancient essence and the inherent potential within you. It is then when your true essence begins to open and flower.

The Key to Relaxation

Simple de-contraction and relaxation open a path to becoming an integral human. Trust the healing power of Nature and allow it to flow into you. It is best not to think about it. This is not a process of, *Well, I am going to think myself into a healing state.* It is a process of opening, relaxing, and allowing the healing power of Nature to enter you. The most important key is to actually trust that it will.

You may remember relaxing in a warm spring meadow where Mother Earth absorbed your tensions, or remember resting in the cool, fresh shade of a forest that calmed your emotional anxiety, or recall being on a mountain, where the spacious view helped all your troubles dissolve in the vast sky. If you can develop this art of relaxing with Nature, it can transform your life. The ability to relax can be brought back into the middle of city living. If relaxation is consciously practiced in the face of powerful urban contractions, it can become the key to mastering the stressful world of modern life.

Relaxation Practice #1: Establishing the Relationship

Begin by finding a place in Nature where you feel comfortable and nurtured. Find a place where you trust the Earth, plants, and sky to help you surrender into deep union of inner and outer nature. Next, find a being of Nature with whom you would like to connect. Perhaps on a walk through the forest you are drawn to a magnificent tree or a peaceful stream. When you find that special place and that being that speaks to your heart, lie down and get comfortable. If needed, you can use a natural fiber blanket, wool or cotton, to lie on or cover you. Synthetic fibers and rubber tend to block much of the Earth's beneficial qi.

Later on you can do relaxation practices in sitting or standing mediation postures. Initially, however, the practice is most effective when you are lying down.

1. Recline on your back with your hands along your sides, feet slightly apart. You may find it helpful to place a rolled towel under your knees to give them a relaxing slight bend.

2. Close your eyes, and relax your diaphragm and abdomen.

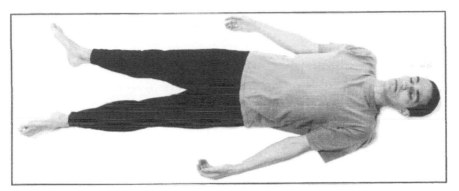

Deep relaxation posture

3. Slowly feel yourself beginning to let go. Breathe softly and deeply into your belly, gently releasing all stress into Mother Earth. Visualize your released blockages to be like fertilizer for her; she transforms them into free, vital Earth qi.

4. Notice the places in your body where you feel contracted. Then consciously bring in a feeling of warmth and trust. Trust that the beings of nature are there to help you, work with you, and share their healing energy.

Please take note and remember that all these beings are not inert. They are living, organic beings just like you. The difference is this: These beings have lived in harmony with all of Nature and all of the Earth for millions of years. They live in a state of harmony and balance that has much to offer you, particularly if your life is out of balance and harmony with your inner self and with Nature. These beings can help bring you back into natural equilibrium and unity with yourself and all of Nature, so trust that insight.

Over time, with repeated sessions of this practice, you will refine your awareness of expanding relaxation. You will find yourself capable of feeling into aspects of your body, from surface to core, that were previously quite insensitive, shielded, or blocked. If unattended, these blockages can lead to lowered vitality, an impoverished quality of life, and illnesses of many kinds. Remember that your contractions may have many sources, but they usually arise from strong emotions such as fear, anger, sadness, anxiety, and worry. Recall that by doing this practice, supported by Nature, you can help powerfully transform these negative emotions.

Communing with a Tree

First, before you do anything, find a tree that you would like to commune with. Ask its permission to come together in deeper relationship. When you feel you have been accepted, you can begin. Amazing and powerful experiences can arise by simply sitting, open and receptive, with your back against a tree. Better yet, stand firmly rooted and embrace the tree like an old friend not seen for a long time. As you sense into the tree you may experience the impression of being held by a loving embrace. As that begins to happen, begin the natural process of letting go of your accumulated tensions.

Once you have established your relationship with this tree, you may begin to feel a deep communion together that makes it easy for you to trust the kind of healing energy that begins to open. Trust yourself to let go of the contractions and tensions that you have been holding.

A tree is extremely centered in its being and is well grounded and rooted. It is at one with the sky above and the earth below. As you connect with this tree, by direct demonstration, it offers you this lesson. In a sense, the tree transmits this utterly grounded way of being directly into you. Just as the tree crown lifts to the heavens, feel your spirit opening and flowering into the vastness and spaciousness of the sky. At the same time, feel yourself completely rooted and deeply connected with Mother Earth.

The tree does not need to move around. It is totally centered in its place. You can find that same kind of center in yourself, wherever you are, if you are simply reminded of what it feels like when you lean against the tree or give the tree a wonderful hug.

You can ask for the spiritual and healing energy of the tree to flow into you, teach you, and help heal you. This is a simple, uncomplicated thing to do. Of course, this power applies to all the beings of Nature. All Creation's beings have this capacity to connect you with the primal.

For example, I've had extraordinary experiences while lying down in fields of wildflowers near my alpine home in the southern Rocky Mountains. At high elevations of eleven thousand to twelve thousand feet, we have amazing fields of wildflowers that unfold for miles. I recall many times lying down in these radiant meadows when I felt tense, out of balance, and very blocked. I have incredible memories of the powerful presence of those flowers, feeling the energy of those wildflower fields completely merging with me and elevating my whole being into bliss.

Trust the process of completely letting go and surrendering to what the plants, animals, rocks, and elements of Gaia have to give you. This may sound like something special, but in truth, anyone can experience this. Nature stands ready to help anyone who opens themselves to the gifts that she has to bring. All you need to do is open yourself to her help and be present for what is given, with no expectations. Relax into the experience. Remember that your tensions and blockages only serve as barriers to Gaia's grace.

Yet, if you are willing to relax into Nature, the healing power of Nature will flow into your entire being.

Whether you believe in this process of relationship or not, it will still work to some degree. Relationship to Mother Earth happens for anyone, even cynics and those who rape the wilderness. However, if you open yourself to intending real relationship with some member of Gaia's family, powerful communion with that being is much more likely. Your heart and mind can help support the opening process. So trust the healing power of Nature, open, and let it flow through you.

In the Native American way, Great Spirit is seen flowing through all the beings of Nature, including you. Birds, plants, stones, mammals, mountains—all are seen as your relatives. For this reason, most Native American prayers include giving thanks to all Creation in this profoundly ecological phrase: "I give thanks to all my relations."

Relaxation Practice #2: Body Scan Relaxation

The following series of exercises involve using your awareness to scan through your body—first to discover where you are holding tension, then to relax the contractions you found, and finally to bring your awareness into your organ, circulatory, nervous, and meridian systems.

Abdominal Breathing

As you do any relaxation or meditation exercise, it is important to maintain deep abdominal breathing throughout the practice. It is incredible how much tension most of us hold abdominally. Because we hold the muscles of the belly and diaphragm tight, many people have limited ability to breathe deeply into the belly. By breathing in a shallow way, we have lost the ability to massage the internal organs of the lower torso with our breath. We tend to breathe only with a shallow kind of upper chest breath. If you ask somebody to demonstrate their normal breathing, often they will breathe by deeply puffing up the chest, but the abdominal area will not move at all.

There are external cultural reasons that men and women breathe incorrectly. Men are taught to stand like a marine, so they pull back their shoulders, suck in their gut, and push their chest out. Women have also been taught the same cultural body blockage. Women are taught that it is beautiful to have a small waist, so they tuck in the abdominal muscles, breathe from the chest, and thrust out the upper torso to show off the breasts. In addition to all these insults, women periodically have to walk in high heels to display long legs, leaving their bodies ungrounded and legs and feet unstable.

One of the main internal reasons for shallow breathing is unresolved anxiety and other painful emotions that are stuffed and frozen into the lower torso. Deep breathing is avoided because this would start to open up these painful feelings for re-experience. Shallow breathing helps assure they will stay safely repressed and inaccessible. Paradoxically, once you begin to breathe deeply into this repressed territory, the emotions and the blocked energy held with them are released and transformed. The main secret for transforming blocked emotions is to breathe deeply and gently into them while applying the first and second principles, relaxation and presence. When you start to move the emotional/energetic blockage out with the breath, free energy then becomes available. Your practice is to simply stay clearly present with the feeling of it, while at the same time relaxing into its core. Ultimately, when this unblocking process is correctly applied, the emotional blockage must dissolve and transform into liberated life force.

Until you can breathe in this way, there is little hope for spiritual progress, so please honor the path of liberating your emotional demons and practice relaxed breathing with patience and diligence.

If you watch the way a baby breathes, you will notice the whole musculature of the abdomen is completely open and participating in the breathing process. You want to breathe just like a baby, deeply into the belly and including the chest area.

If you are having difficulty learning how to focus on correct abdominal breathing, you may find it helpful to lie down. The diaphragm naturally relaxes when one is prone, and the breath is able to sink. After you master deep belly breathing lying down, you can practice the belly breathing sitting or standing.

Observing

During this phase you will be scanning through your body to notice where you are holding tension. This first phase is only for observing where contractions are found in your body.

- Go out into your favorite place in nature—a place where you feel nature supporting you to de-contract, relax, and let go. If weather allows, go barefoot, or wear cotton or leather-soled moccasins so that your feet can feel Mother Earth.

- Recline on your back with your hands along your sides, feet slightly apart. If you find it helpful, you can place a rolled towel under your knees to give them a relaxed, supportive bend.

- Close your eyes.

- Relax your diaphragm and abdomen. Breathe softly and deeply into your belly.

- Begin the scan. With relaxed awareness, you will be peacefully scanning your whole body, from your head to the soles of your feet. Pay attention to where the contractions are. Where are you holding and blocking your energy? Consider this practice an exploration of inner nature with the support of that beautiful, natural place outdoors, ready to help you soften those stiff areas of the body. What you observe may not appear to you as something that is tense; you may only notice a slight discomfort. Initially you are just allowing your body to express what it is experiencing. Simply spend time noticing and making friends with your body.

- Begin by shifting your awareness to the crown of your head.

- Pay attention to how your body feels as you slowly scan down through all the facial muscles and the scalp.

- Be aware of the muscles of your jaw and then scan down through the throat.

- Move your awareness through the muscles in the neck.

- Scan the shoulders and arms.

- Gently bring your attention to the area of the hands and the fingers.

- Next, scan the upper back and the upper front of the body, including the upper chest.

- Continue to scan down through the lower chest, central abdomen, and middle back.

- Scan down through the lower back and the lower abdomen.

- Scan the sides of the body.

- Pay attention to any contractions as your intention moves into the pelvic area.

- Notice any tension in the genitals, anal area, and perineum.

- Scan down through each of the legs and down into the soles of the feet.

Relaxing

Many people believe learning how to relax the physical, energetic, and emotional blockages in their bodies is something extremely difficult and challenging. In truth, it is no more difficult than taking a tightened fist and intending to relax it. For example, sit down at a table and rest your arm on it. Make a tight fist. Then, with your intention, naturally and gently open your clenched fist into a relaxed open-palmed hand. Now do the same thing with every part of your body. If you are not sure it is working, do not worry about it. Your worries create more contraction. Trust your intention to guide the de-contraction and relaxation process. Simply know that it is happening. Day by day, as you practice this relaxation process, it will reveal aspects of your being that you never knew were contracted and blocked. In the beginning, simply intend this deep relaxation and trust that it will happen.

You cannot force relaxation. The attempt to force relaxation just creates more contraction. Simply bring your awareness into the places that you feel tension in your body. Gently feel the tension in those areas soften and dissolve. Be aware of your tendency to get frustrated or distracted. If your mind wanders, gently bring it back to the intention of relaxing all the constricted, tight, or stiff blockages. Your frustration is completely counterproductive. You will create more tension and more anxiety. Be patient and allow Nature to take its course. Go with the natural flow of this process of relaxation from the crown of the head down to the soles of the feet, and let it happen in a spontaneous and gentle way.

Now that you have scanned your whole body and discovered where you are holding contractedness, you can apply the same observation skills you have learned to actually relax your entire body. Wherever you feel any tension, allow your mind to rest with that tension and gently relax into it. Let it soften. Feel a sense of natural ease beginning to replace your feelings of tension and anxiety. As you go through this process, feel the incredible support of Mother Earth merging with you from below.

During this phase you will focus on releasing tensions. You discover how Nature's fresh qi replaces the blocked life force. So, scan your body again, beginning at the crown of your head and moving all the way down to the soles of your feet. Use the outline from the "Observing" section to guide your awareness through the entire body.

Trust the healing power of Nature to flow into you to help with the relaxation process and opening process. Do not worry about whether it is working or not. Feel the muscles softening, loosening, opening, and relaxing. Your face may begin to feel warm. You may also experience a sensation that your muscles actually feel happy as they open and relax. Enjoy the sensation of clean, clear energy arising throughout your being.

Giving Your Tension to Mother Earth

Feel these tensions and blockages pouring out of you down into Mother Earth. Feel all the contractions being absorbed by Mother Earth. See Mother Earth receiving them as fertilizer. Mother Earth can take anything and transform it. She can take any kind of tension, blockage, or waste material and turn it into beautiful, fertile soil. If you are practicing along a stream, feel the tension melting out into the energy flow of the stream as you visualize it pouring in through you. Once in the stream, see the contracted energy transformed into positive qi by the powerful qi of the stream. Similarly, if you are in a field of flowers, feel the flowers naturally helping to transform the blockages. If you are practicing with a tree, feel the wonderful tree open a deep centeredness and natural flowing connection in you between Heaven and Earth, which allows you to release the tensions. Again visualize Gaia transmuting all toxicity into clear, free life force. Once you release the blockages, you will experience a feeling of deep relaxation as the inflow of fresh life force replaces your blocked life force.

Deeper Relaxation

As you become familiar with the process of your body scan, you can use this exercise to send fresh, positive qi flowing through other systems of your body.

- Scan through your body and relax all of the organs. Make sure to include your brain, heart, stomach, pancreas, gall bladder, lungs, liver, kidneys, and sexual organs.

- Scan through your body and relax all the elements of the nervous system. Emphasize the nerves and their connection to your spinal column.

- Scan through your body and relax through the circulatory system. Feel the blood move through all of your arteries, veins, and capillaries.

- Again, as you relax, feel the rejuvenating life force of Nature flow into you and revitalize you.

I would recommend concluding with a practice of scanning down through the qi channels and meridians of the whole body. You do not have to know where the channels and meridians exactly are. These energy pathways flow just on the surface of the body. All you have to do is scan the entire body surface with the intention to relax and open all of the qi pathways so that they are open, smooth, and flowing. If you are familiar with the locations of the energy chakras[1] of your body, you can include them when you do your final body scan.

After you complete the body scan relaxation practice, your awareness of the body should be that it is completely purified, relaxed, opened, and rejuvenated. Delight in the restorative power of the Earth and all her beings. Appreciate all of the gifts of healing that you have received. Radiate back your appreciation for all these healing gifts. Remain in this renewed state of natural, open, spacious, profound surrender until you wish to rise. This is the way of opening up to receiving all the gifts and blessings of Nature. It is the doorway to a very sacred view of you and of the Earth. It can provide you with a deep experience of your true nature and the Great Mystery of what we call Earth and the cosmos. Do this practice once or twice a day and it will bring many benefits.

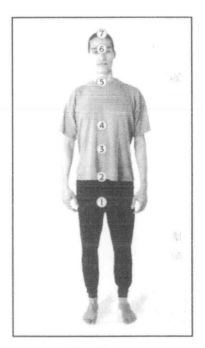

The Chakras

Dedication to Practice

Over a period of days, weeks, months, and years, you will discover layers of shielding, contrac-

---

1. Chakra—in Yoga, a chakra is any one of the centers (or "wheels") of spiritual power in the human body. According to which system is used, there may be five, seven, nine, or more main chakras associated with the human form. In all systems, each of the body's main chakras is associated with specific energetic qualities.

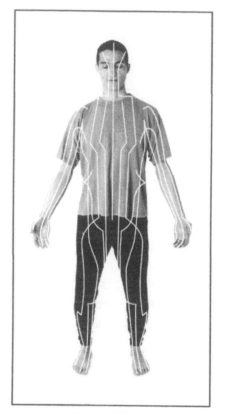

Qi Meridians

tion, tension, anxiety, and separation you never dreamed you could have possibly been holding. Be patient with your relaxation practice. Remember that these layers of separation and contraction that shield and block you from resting in a relaxed state, take time to be revealed and released. Because these layers have blocked you from fully living your life, once they begin to dissolve and wash away you will start opening to a magnificent world that may seem miraculous. You may ask, *How could I have not seen this before?*

The flower of your true nature is no different from the tremendous gift of outer Nature, of the wild, which is already in balance and harmony. Wilderness is already perfectly integrated. As you discover your integral being, you will be supported by the primal integral being of Gaia. She nourishes you as you go through your practice.

Presence

A WONDERFUL LINE FROM THE BUDDHIST DZOGCHEN Tantras states that pure awareness of nowness is the real Buddha, which means surrendering completely into pure presence. The essence of pure presence is the essence of all the enlightened and liberated beings who have ever existed. Presence is one of the most direct, immediate qualities of the liberated state.

It is interesting that our culture makes it extremely difficult to cultivate authentic presence. There are so many distractions in our society that pull us away from being fully in the now. Our friends, family, and all the demands of a daily work routine pull us away from living in the moment. Paradoxically, all the work and striving is usually done to open up a little space and time to enjoy life. We work very hard to save time, and yet we have very little time to enjoy the life for which we are saving time!

Many of the great liberated beings realized that unless you make a deep commitment to embracing pure presence right now in whatever you are doing, there is little hope of really enjoying life and going beyond into the deeper openings of the liberated state. Presence is at the heart of The Way of Nature principles. Genuine presence provides a natural path of liberation in Nature.

Presence with Relaxation

In many ways the union of presence and relaxation is the key to spiritual practice. Becoming pristinely present while in a state of deep relaxation, totally surrendered to the moment, is the heart of spiritual practice in Nature. When we combine presence with relaxation there is a kind of alchemy, or fusion, that occurs. Presence and relaxation merge into a union of alive openness and relaxed surrender.

If you go deeply into surrender without heightened presence, there is a tendency to fall asleep. If you move into a sense of heightened presence only, without relaxation and surrender, there is a tendency to become tense and anxious. Have you ever noticed when you slowly sound out the word *attention* it becomes *a-tension?* Attention without relaxation causes the presence aspect to become tense and actually begins to move you back into a contracted state. If you merge presence with relaxation, the two come together in a beautiful way to support each other and the opening of the natural state of mind.

Distraction

Most of us are not only contracted, but we are also distracted. The realization of our distracted state shows us the importance of presence in our lives. If you do not honor the truth of your distractedness, then it is difficult to make progress dissolving those distractions. Any movement toward becoming more present must first acknowledge the truth of how distracted you are now.

The first step to noticing the level of your distractedness is to start paying attention to how often your mind wanders off into things that have nothing to do with the here and now. Pay attention to how your mind drifts away into things that happened in the past, or worries about things that may arise in the future. Noticing our tendency to move away from the now into thoughts of past and future make us aware of how little time we are spending in the here and now. At first, as you notice the basic distractedness of your thoughts and emotions, it might be quite overwhelming to discover what little time you are spending right here, in the awareness of nowness.

Early Lessons in Presence

When I first started practicing zazen, a Japanese Buddhist-style meditation, as a teenager back in the 1950s, it amazed me that I carried so much tension and distraction. I had a good teacher who helped me through many difficult times dealing with some of the adolescent tensions many of us carry at that age. The most effective thing for me was combining meditation practice with my vision quests and solo journeys into wild Nature. These journeys allowed me to unravel a lot of my own distractions and tensions at a rapid pace.

I am still incredibly thankful to my first meditation teacher, Ed Maupin. He gave me some great gifts. Ed had studied in a Zen monastery in Japan. He came to the United States to share some of those teachings and complete one of the earliest studies of the psychological effects of Buddhist meditation on practitioners. I volunteered to be one of his experimental subjects at the University of Michigan. It was extremely rare to run across anyone who meditated in the United States during that era. Zazen was not even heard of. Even Yoga practitioners were rare. Nobody talked about or seemed interested in Buddhist, Taoist, or Hindu-style meditation. All of these things were unknown for most of us in contemporary American culture at that time. Therefore, I did not have a whole lot of company for my practice, but what I did have was Nature. Combining the practice of being in Nature with the zazen meditation guidance from Ed was tremendously helpful, and I am very thankful to him. It also planted the seeds of what was to become a lifelong process of distilling common principles and practices found from Earth-connected and liberating traditions.

The Great Feline Meditator

In the mornings I often spend a little time with our cat, Lionel. He is one of the greatest meditators I have come across. He can sit in a state of absolutely still, pure presence for hours. If there is even a slight movement of somebody in the room, or if I am in bed and turn over, he is immediately aware of the movement. He is totally in the now. Lionel seems to not be distracted by trance states. He is not distracted by thoughts. He is just there for whatever is happening, but he is resting completely in that state of pure nowness.

Many beings of Nature carry that state of pure presence. They carry it naturally in their being. Therefore, plants and animals can be great teachers for us when we spend time with them. They are not caught up in distractions about past and future. They know how to enjoy the here and now. They know how to live fully and joyfully in the moment. When you spend time with trees, flowers, birds, and other animals—which all carry the great teachings of being in the now—you can receive some great instruction. These gifts will come naturally and flow into your heart. You will begin to be able to relax and trust being present, instead of fighting it.

Nature Supports Presence

Nature can support being more present. As a basic practice of presence you might try gazing into the mountains or forest and being with the sound of the birds flying through the sky. Feel the touch of the wind on your body. Feel the warmth of the Sun opening and relaxing your whole being. Living outdoors provides a wonderful environment in which to open, relax, and surrender into the quality of pure presence.

Nature can aid the process of recognizing our distractedness. Going into Nature, even for a short time each day, and sitting or standing quietly will help reduce distraction. Pay attention to the beauty of the trees, the flow of the water, the shimmering quality of the light in the sky, the curl of a cloud moving through the vast blue heavens, or a bird dipping to drink from a pond nearby. All wonderful things that you see in Nature occur in the immeasurable present moment. Nature gives us endless opportunities to surrender into the beauty of now and how it is unfolding. Nature gives us opportunities to be in a spontaneous meditative state in which we move with the flow of Nature. We blend with how Nature is naturally arising. This is a powerful practice.

One of my favorite things to do is to go into a forest, to a mountain, or by a river or wild coast and spend an hour or two each day. I will slowly and intentionally walk a little bit, then stop and sit quietly with attention to the silence, beauty, and tranquility. This practice allows me to appreciate tranquility within myself, inspired by the incredible beauty and innate harmony of outer nature. The movement of the mind easily slows down. The busyness of thoughts regarding the past and future dissolve and wash away. You will find yourself coming into the here and now because truth surrounds you. All of Nature supports your being in the present moment. You do not even have to meditate. You can simply enjoy being in Nature. A natural state of unity with the present moment arises when you surrender to the awesome embrace of Gaia, and a spontaneous kind of meditation begins to happen. When you move into that state, there is an effortless union of your own inner nature with outer nature. The inner and outer begin to naturally come together without any artifice, contrivance, or special practices.

Breaking the Habit of Distraction

To begin seeing benefits from cultivating presence, it is important to commit to spending time each day simply being in a natural setting in a space where you are not preoccupied with the busyness of the rest of your life. This new pattern of behavior provides you with the opportunity to learn how to unwind the habit of constantly being in a distracted state of mind. Most of us are literally habituated to distraction, making it difficult to unwind. I often repeat to my students, "Make habit your friend." By committing to becoming more present, supported by your pledge to go into Nature for a little time each day, you will be able to venture a lot deeper into the experience. Make this practice of being intimately now with Nature your new, spiritually supportive habit. If you have a lot of time to really enjoy being in Nature, then you could discover that presence is actually not what you might have thought. The quality of presence can be refined. You can go deeper and deeper into a precise nowness that has infinite depth.

In a single second, many things pass through most people's minds; at a subtle level, they are not even aware of these effervescent thoughts. As you begin to spend more time being present, you will start to notice subtle qualities that arise, appear, and then vanish from your mind. As you spend more time refining moment-centered awareness, you will find that many of the things that were subtle distractions will begin to dissolve and fall away and your sense of each unique instant will continue to deepen.

As this sense of presence increases, feelings of bliss, joy, and happiness will begin to appear. These feelings are great gifts that come along with this kind of self-cultivation. Ultimately, you will find yourself being able to spend long periods of time resting in a sense of clear now without any particular thoughts marring that state. If thoughts do arise, you experience them arising out of pure nowness, manifesting in pure nowness, and dissolving back into pure nowness, moment by moment. When this level of presence begins to manifest for you in a natural flow, it is one of life's greatest insights. This is what the Tibetan Dzogchen texts are referring to when they say that presence, the pure awareness of nowness, is the real Buddha. All beings carry as their ultimate essence pure Buddha Nature, this pure essence of nowness.

Breaking the Habits of Worry and Anxiety

Most of us, because of the busyness of our minds, are quite attached to our worries. What would we do without them? We worry about how things are going to go in the future and stew over what we have done in the past. We may feel guilt, anxiety, or regret because of things that happened in the past. We may still be carrying a lot of grief or sadness. This is all heavy baggage. The cure for much worry and anxiety is the cultivation of presence. We do not have to continue as the victims of our negative emotions and thoughts. As I mentioned above, we have developed the habit of allowing these distractions from past and future to dominate our feelings and thoughts. These habits are like a self-imposed tyranny—troubling interpretations of the past and projections or speculations about the future that completely take us over. Consequently, I recommend developing an alternative habit by dedicating, at least several times a day, ten, twenty, or more minutes in Nature, and totally devote this special time to being present and enjoying the here and now. The moment you begin to find your mind wandering off into future or past, immediately recognize it and bring yourself back into an appreciation of the current moment. Combining this new behavior with some simple meditative practices (described later) can help you surrender even more deeply into your experience of each extraordinary instant. Nothing like this moment has ever happened before. Nothing like this instant will ever happen again.

Even without meditative practice, if you are flowing in a state of continuous nowness in Nature, you are cultivating a tremendous antidote to counter the normal distractedness of our culture. You can bring this present-centered awareness back into your ordinary life, and you will find that the flow of your normal day will gradually become transformed. You will find that instead of spending each precious moment of your life being distracted by worry and concern about the past and future, you will be able to focus on the one true thing—that which arises each instant. You can go deeply into a current issue, work with it, deal with it in the moment, and then move on to the next thing and the next instant, without being overwhelmed by distractions.

A Mind Like a Ferris Wheel

The number one issue for many of the participants who come to experience one of my Sacred Passage programs is the waterfall of distractions that tumble over them. A few years ago, a man came to my Chiricahua mountain retreat cabin from the Garment District of New York. For the sake of telling his story, I'll call him Ben. He spent four days doing Awareness Training with me, and then went out to be alone in the mountains to practice the Awareness Training teachings. The plan was for Ben to spend three or four days alone, integrating the meditative practices I had taught. I would remain at the cabin, close by to his vision quest camp, to be there should he need me.

The day after he entered his solo, I went to do errands in a small village, Elfrida, about twenty-five miles away. After finishing my errands, I started back to the cabin. As I was getting in my car to drive back, I looked up and saw Ben walking down the tiny main street of little Elfrida.

I went over to him and asked, "What happened?"

Ben replied, "John, I'm terribly sorry but it was incredible. Incredible! I had no idea."

"You had no idea of what?" I asked.

"I had no idea of how incredibly busy and distracted my mind was. It was like a Ferris wheel. It never stopped moving. It was constantly churning ideas, concepts, worries, and concerns. I was caught in a torrent of thoughts. I could only think about things I had done in the past and things I wanted to do in the future. It just never stopped. I had no idea my mind was like that. I had to leave. It was too much. My mind was driving me crazy."

I responded, "Well, is your mind any calmer now?"

He looked at me and said, "Oh!"

We talked and he realized that he tended to cover over the normal tension and distractedness of his being by surrounding himself with a lot of busyness in the outer world. This was actually the first time he had ever stopped long enough to become aware of this waterfall of anxious, intense thoughts and distractions that were constantly flowing through his being and sapping his energy.

He expressed, "You know, I thought that I was developing a problem out there, but actually what I realize after we've gone through this, what I've realized is that actually all that stuff was there all along, it's just that this is the first time that I realized it was there."

I remarked, "Do you realize that you have had a tremendous breakthrough? This is the first time in your life that you have been aware of what has been going on all the time. Up until now, it has remained hidden away in your psyche. It has been sapping your strength, energy, and ability to relax and be present. Your distractions and contractions have conspired to destroy your ability to enjoy life. But don't be too tense about suddenly trying to turn all this around. Do not try to change this pattern overnight. Rather, in a natural and relaxed way, start doing that simple meditation I shared with you during the Awareness Training. You remember that practice? Each day spend some time just being fully present with what is going on in your life, and spend a little daily time meditating in Nature just the way I showed you."

He came back with me to the mountains and reentered his vision quest solo, on a modified basis, and was able to complete it.

I touched base with Ben a few years later. He reflected on his experiences since that day. He said:

John, that Sacred Passage absolutely transformed my life. That was one of the major turning points in my life. It opened up a whole new way of being that I had had no concept of. I grew up in the craziness of the New York Garment District. We are all intensely busy over here, and we always have way too much to do. Our minds are running all the time. Tension is everywhere. I came to you with no background for seeing how distracted I was. Meditation was just a word. Nature was something strange and unfamiliar, something "out there." I had no idea that this way of being, this relaxation and present-centered life, was even possible. Now, everything has changed. Joy is flowing back into my days. Thank you.

Ben's experience is not uncommon. However, he may have been an extreme example of somebody who was totally caught up in the anxious flow of continuous thought. He had mastered the ability to be in a state of continuous distraction. All we did together was open up the other possibility of becoming a master of pure presence. I always think of Ben when I teach the concept of presence because his honesty was so beautiful. I loved the direct, almost childlike way he shared the description of his mind as a Ferris wheel or a waterfall of continuous, anxious thoughts. He shared his experience with such innocence and truth that it opened the door to total transformation of his life.

Eye of the Eagle

The goal of a Native American–style vision quest is to go into Nature in a sacred way to make a deep connection with one's essence and with Mother Earth, and to realize pure vision. A traditional vision quest is unlike our contemporary Way of Nature's Sacred Passage. With Sacred Passage, one usually solos a few days longer, for seven days. The "passager's" goal is an experience of profound communion with Gaia, and clearing the path for a major realization of Source awareness. As the passage unfolds, one attains a powerful connection to the unique purpose of the soul's current incarnation. The passage process is gentler — suitable even for beginners in spiritual practice and camping in Nature. Each person can have a tent, sleeping bag, water, clothing, and a sacred circle of either 108 feet or 108 yards in diameter and can even take light food. Sacred Passage preparation requires only two to four weeks beforehand. The five to seven days of the Awareness Training unfolds immediately before and after the solo.

By contrast, when I guide a traditional vision quest, the aspirant prepares for many months, up to a year, before starting. Ideally, they will have undertaken at least several Sacred Passages as part of their preparation. During the four- or five-day solo, there is no food, little or no water, no tent, no clothing, only a blanket or the equivalent, and no sleep. The vision quester alternates between prayer, meditation, ceremony, and energy practices that support the process. One stays within a sacred circle of only eight feet in diameter the entire time. The process is quite rigorous, and spiritually, emotionally, and physically demanding.

The following story is a personal vision quest experience, which illustrates presence in Nature quite well. It happened in the early 1980s during a wilderness solo in the Sangre de Cristo Mountains, above the little town of Crestone in southern Colorado. My vision quest site was in a very sacred area, on a summit of a lofty, bald peak. In this case, I was following many of the practices used in this ancient Native American–style rite of passage. I was up on a treeless, rounded summit of about twelve thousand feet overlooking the San Luis Valley, a large, level valley seventy-five hundred feet high between the Sangre de Cristo and San Juan Mountains. I had been meditating on and off with Nature for several days, allowing present-centered awareness to help me merge with the forest below, the soaring mountains all around me, and the infinity of sky above. One afternoon I meditated atop a rocky outcrop on the edge of a cliff. Below me was a forested valley canyon, clothed with aspens and adorned with cliffs rising here and there above the trees. Overall, the canyon was quite steep. While sitting, I suddenly noticed a slight movement off to my right. I glanced and saw beneath me, flying clearly above the aspen trees, a beautiful bald eagle. It was flying due east, the direction of spiritual awakening, and was perhaps only several hundred feet below. This was an unusual thing to see in that part of the world. The Crestone region primarily has golden eagles. Here, however, there was no mistake. With its unambiguous markings, a bald eagle was flying free and clear, directly beneath me.

The eagle had its wings outstretched in a long glide. It was soaring directly below me so that I was able to look down on the top of its back. It turned its head a bit and glanced up at me. Then it brought its head back down and continued to glide up the canyon toward the mountain. I was quite close to the eagle and could see a lot of detail. It was amazingly beautiful. The golden brown and snowy white on its back and the sharply defined beak were striking. As I gazed down, I could not believe I was actually seeing it. I blinked and in that moment the eagle was gone, vanished.

In the next instant, I felt tremendous energy and a pull from the west. I turned my head west and saw what appeared to be the same bald eagle about a half mile away. At that time, the Sun was setting, a glowing orange-red ball hanging low in the sky, across the San Luis Valley. The Sun was slightly above the horizon. I was stunned. In the blink of my eye the eagle had somehow transported itself a half mile in the opposite direction and was now corkscrewing directly upward into the shimmering disk of the Sun. It penetrated into the circle of the Sun. When the eagle reached the center of the Sun disk, it turned, reset its wings, and went into a steep dive out of the Sun straight as an arrow toward me. It flew directly over my head, and I could feel the energy of the eagle bless me as it passed close overhead. The energy penetrated and filled every cell of my being. Then it flew beyond me and disappeared to the east, in the high peaks of the Sangre de Cristos behind me.

Needless to say, I was totally awestruck by the experience. I literally fell over backwards from my meditation posture as the eagle passed over my head. The flat rock cradled me as I fell. I lay there for a long time, completely saturated with the incredible transmission of eagle energy—pure eagle spirit.

As I lay there, a cloud began to form and pass over my vision quest site. I looked into the sky and realized that I was staring up into the form of a giant cloud-eagle. The cloud had taken the identical shape of the eagle that had passed over me moments before, but on a massive scale. The cloud-eagle was probably several miles across with perfect white tail feathers, widespread wings, feet with claws, and a large head with beak.

The eyes of the cloud-eagle were amazing. As it passed above me the eyes were formed by two huge circular holes that were open and empty, right through the eagle head of the cloud. I found myself gazing into the eagle's eyes, which carried me into the vast and empty clear space of the sky. At that moment I felt something transmitted to me. It is difficult to put the experience into words. At that moment, everything dissolved. I was gone, the cloud-eagle was gone, and the mountains were gone. The only thing left was an incredible incandescent luminosity and a vast, clear, empty space. This space was much like the vastness of the sky but even more expansive than that. It was the vastness of absolute pure presence. The clear light of pure, spacious awareness dawned.

I remained in that state for a very long time. When I came back into normal consciousness, the cloud-eagle was still there but it had passed in the same direction that the first eagle had gone— east toward the mountain. Finally, it dissolved in the sky over the mountains. Not a trace remained.

Because of the vision quest, I had been in a deep meditative state for a number of days. The arrival of the eagle was a tremendous blessing, transmission, and initiation. I was completely at one with the eagle that passed below me, and one with the vast eagle spirit that passed over in the sky above. In the Native American tradition, an eagle signifies direct communion with Great Spirit. Transmissions like this have great significance in the context of a vision quest. This was one of the more powerful initiations I have received from a totem being, as the Native American tradition would describe this eagle. It was an initiation into a very powerful and profound level of presence—an opening into the Great Mystery of pure Source itself.

I wanted to share this story because it illustrates the incredible power that Nature and Great Spirit can bring to anyone who really opens up to these two simple principles, relaxation and presence. The merging of those two qualities was precisely what had been accomplished on top of that cliff, before the eagle came to me.

Awakenings from cultivation of presence and relaxation in Nature can also be subtle. One of the most profound awakenings I have been graced with happened when I was sitting in a marvelous aspen grove. Over several hours, a very refined state of deep and profound presence opened. At the moment when presence was absolutely timeless, an aspen leaf let go from the top of an aspen tree and spiraled down in front of me. The sound of the leaf hitting the ground created a burst of present-centered clarity and luminosity in my being that was extraordinary. This gift came because presence had been refined to a deep level. Anyone can do this. The simplest beings in Nature can help bring the gifts of profound presence and the opening of spacious clear awareness for us all. All we have to do is to commit ourselves to resting in Source awareness, and take the time to do it.

Presence Practices

Cultivation of presence is crucial to spiritual development. There are several exercises that can help you deepen presence. I would highly recommend these exercises be done outdoors in Nature, as the support of Nature will help you deepen your presence tremendously.

Presence Practice #1 — Slow Movement

The first exercise works with very slow movement. When you move in a slow way, it allows you to become aware of where you are holding your tensions and blockages. When this practice is refined, your body, emotions, and mind are all involved in a harmonious process. By slowing down body movement, it becomes clear to us where we lack presence. This process begins to open the doorway to being able to move while being fully in the now.

This exercise has a relationship to sacred dance and some of the Chinese martial arts such as T'ai Chi. Since learning T'ai Chi can take many years for one to gain even minimal competence, I have designed this slow movement meditative practice as something that allows people to have many of the benefits that come from T'ai Chi right from the start. You do not have to be an expert; you can do it any time.

Walking

Select a natural outdoor location for your movement practice. Begin by walking at an extremely slow pace. Instead of walking at your normal rate, slow it down to something like a slow-motion movie speed. This includes the tempo of the arms and the whole body, not just the legs. If you have seen T'ai Chi, try to move your entire body, including the swinging of the arms, at the T'ai Chi pace. After you have done this for three or four minutes, slow it down again to half that tempo. After another five minutes or so, again slow it down to half of that speed.

Allowing inspiration from the movements of Nature is beneficial to this practice. You can be inspired by the way the clouds move in the sky above you. You can be inspired by the way the water in a stream flows around a rock. Let that movement of the water inspire your own movement. Your movement can be inspired by many things in Nature, but remember the main principle of this exercise is to move very slowly.

There is a natural tendency to speed up in the midst of this practice because of impatience to get back to our normal rate of movement. By slowing yourself down every five minutes or so, you move back into that slow-motion speed, which becomes a process of deepening presence while in motion. It is great to do this with a few friends, because you can share the process together and support each other in maintaining the slow rate of movement.

Sitting

A variation of this exercise is to start by sitting. Very slowly lift your arm and let it rise up and slowly sweep in front of you. Move your arm across your body, continuing at a slow pace. As you do this, pay attention to wherever you're holding tension in the arm, hand, fingers, and shoulders. Ideally, move as slowly as a snail moves across a stone. Imagine you are pulling silk out of a cocoon. Try visualizing pulling taffy. You want to pull the taffy not so quickly that it breaks, but not so slowly that it drops on the ground. As you do this movement with your arm, focus first on relaxing the shoulder. Then relax the area of the elbow, followed by relaxing the wrist, hand, and fingers. Use only the absolute minimum effort necessary to make the movement. Feel the difference as you make the movement back and forth. After you've discovered your ability to let go of unneeded tension and distractedness in the physical body, take the same movement and slow it down so that you're moving at an almost imperceptible pace.

Releasing Blockages

As you move at this extremely slow pace, you'll notice little blockages. You will feel a lot of little hesitations or holdings in the movement. All of those things are the tensions, anxieties, and blockages that we've held in our bodies for a long time. After practicing this kind of movement over time, all of those little hesitations and blockages will begin to dissolve, and ultimately melt out of you. You'll find that your movements can become more fluid,

Sitting meditation posture

Sitting meditation posture in a chair

smooth, gentle, and flowing. However, you must first discover where you're holding tension in the first place. Moving slowly is one of the best ways to locate tension in your body. You will not always have to move at an extremely slow speed. You can just do slow-motion movement while paying attention to where the tensions and distractions are located in your body. Release the tension, moment to moment, as you move.

Presence Practice #2—Moving Meditation

This is an excellent exercise to do after you have practiced Presence Practice #1 enough to become fully familiar with slow movement. Throughout the following moving meditation exercise, keep your back both erect and relaxed. Feel as though a string connected to the top of your head suspends you. Imagine the sky supporting you by holding your head from above and allowing you to maintain an upright and balanced equilibrium. You might choose to imagine a silver cord of Spirit lifting up into the sky from the top of your head. As it rises up into the heavens, it provides you with wonderful support. It gives you something that helps the body remain light and buoyant. That cord pulls you up at the same time that the lower pelvis and legs are sinking down into Mother Earth. Relax your pelvis and let it drop into a natural position so that there is little or no tension in the lower back and abdomen. Once again, feel the spine being lengthened by the lifting of the head and the sinking of the legs and pelvis. This visualization elongates the spine in a natural way.

Walking Forward and Backward

While standing, start out by sinking down a little bit and slowly pouring all your weight into the left leg. Step out softly and smoothly with your right leg, placing your right foot down gently with the heel first and roll the sole of your foot down as you visualize the energy of the step spiraling down into the Earth. As you make initial contact, also feel the reciprocal sensation of Mother

Earth's energy rising up into your right foot. Once you touch the ground, shift just enough weight to feel that it is firmly on the ground while most of your weight remains rooted into the Earth, as if you had tree roots growing down into the Earth from your left foot. Then begin to shift by pouring the weight from the left leg into the right leg. As you pour the weight into the right leg, feel the left leg emptying. All of the weight flows out of the left leg and into the right leg. Now, root into the Earth with the right leg. Continue moving in this manner. Remain totally present with the feeling of the weight flowing from one leg into the other, and the connection with Mother Earth as you do this. Be present with every moment of that flow. Continue stepping in this manner.

- Throughout the exercise be present with the feeling of rooted connection with Mother Earth. Feel as if each step is like kissing the Earth with your foot.

- During this exercise you can move forward or backward. If you are moving backward, you will be stepping back with your toes touching first, then slowly rolling the weight into the heel of the foot.

Adding Arm Movements

Remain present with a relaxed erectness of the spine, lifting of the crown, and sinking of the pelvis and legs. Continue to root through your feet down into the Earth. Now become aware of your arms. Allow your arms and shoulders to be very relaxed. Let your elbows bend with a relaxed heavy feeling as they sink toward the Earth. The wrists and fingers remain relaxed but open. Let your arms creatively express whatever kind of slow movement you would like to do. Let the movement be inspired by the way the water flows, the way a cloud swirls, or the way a tree sways. Perhaps you've watched a big cat move and you're inspired to move like a cat. Continue moving your arms as you begin to start walking forward and backward again.

Turning from the Pelvis

After walking in a straight line for a while, begin to introduce turning into your movements. When turning, let the pelvis rotate the foot of your unweighted foot to the outside (i.e., if your right foot is stepping forward, then the foot is rotated to the right). The pelvis determines the direction of the turn rather than the head or upper body. Continue the movement by setting the unweighted foot down slowly as before, allowing the weight to flow into it gradually. The rotation from the lower body pulls your rear leg around to the new direction as determined by the pelvis. It is especially important to maintain presence during changes of direction in your movement. It is the integration of pelvic rotation and smooth weight transfer that allows for easy meditative movement while you're turning.

Completing the Practice with Standing Meditation

Standing meditation is one of the most profound practices from the Chinese tradition. A practice that is helpful in all sacred movement systems is to begin and end the movement with a standing meditation. You can also alternate standing meditation with slow movement, and then come back to standing meditation in an ongoing process. At the conclusion of your practice, spend a few minutes to a half hour in the standing posture described below.

- Stand comfortably with heels together and toes turned out to form a "v" shape with the feet

- Weight is evenly distributed between the feet and sinks into the Earth

- Knees are slightly unlocked

- Arms hang relaxed alongside the body

- Pelvis and lower back are relaxed into a natural posture

- Head and spine are upright as if the head is suspended from above

- The tongue touches the upper palate above the upper front teeth

- Breathing is abdominal, done naturally through the nose—soft, smooth, and fine

- Eyes look down at a forty-five-degree angle, paying attention to the whole visual field

- The mind's awareness rests in your lower abdomen, in the lower *tantien*[2]

As you stand, feel through your whole body and notice where you may be tense or contracted. Observe the mind and pay attention when your awareness starts to wander off into a distracted state. Keep yourself in the present moment by noticing exactly what you are feeling in your body. Do a simple body scan by feel-

---

2. This specific area of the lower abdomen is known as the lower tantien (the field of the elixir) in China. The word is often pronounced "Dan Tien." It is technically located the width of your three middle fingers (two to three inches) below the bellybutton and approximately one-third of the way into the body, front to back. The tantien is a natural storage area for human vital energy, or qi. It is one of the most important and safest places to gather the vital energy of the body. It has been compared to a vast ocean of qi within.

ing from the crown of your head down to the soles of your feet. Relax each area where you notice tension. Emphasize presence with each part of the body that is experiencing tension or contraction. In addition, at all times keep some of your awareness in the tantien, in the area of the lower abdomen.

The Support of Nature

Do standing and moving meditation practices outdoors whenever possible. The emphasis is on being present with your body while also realizing your interconnectedness with sky, Earth, and the perceptions of Nature that are coming to you. Be present with whatever things are appearing before you, whether it is a tree or a field of flowers. Notice the touch of the wind on your skin. Pay attention to the smell of the pine trees. Allow the song of the stream to grace inner clarity. Be present with whatever gifts Nature provides to you through your senses.

Bringing Practice Back to Everyday Life

In your everyday life do your best to maintain some sense of slow, relaxed movement. Become aware of how you tend to hold a lot of contractions, distractions, and a lack of presence in your everyday life. For the most part, we carry numerous distractions even in the way we move about our house, do our job, or drive our car. For example, you may discover that you drive with a tremendous amount of unnecessary tension in your shoulders, and that your mind is everywhere but on the road. You may find that when you write at the office you grasp the pen with tension, and that your mind can't focus.

But you do have a choice. You can choose to let the tension go. You can choose to concentrate your mind on the road ahead. You can decide to practice writing with the minimum amount of effort you need. You can train the distracted consciousness to simplify and just center on precisely what is before you. You can choose to be totally present with what you're doing. If you follow the process of paying attention to the present moment in daily activities, everything you do during the flow of the day can be a teacher for you.

I strongly recommend that you practice meditation for at least a half hour, twice a day. The simple Buddhist/Taoist practice of placing the mind on each in-breath is an excellent way for you to begin training your mind. Without such training, your mind will never stop behaving like a wild puppy. However, once you take the time to concentrate your mind on whatever meditation object you choose, then its puppy-like tendency to be constantly distracted will begin to settle. As the mind settles into itself, distractions lose their power over you and natural inner tranquility begins to take the place of constant distractedness. Ultimately, true presence arises from the core of your being. But in the beginning, regular meditation practice is the key. If you cultivate meditation practices in Nature each day, you will further deepen your practice. The harmonious flow of continuous change in Nature is a superb focus for your meditation. You may choose to place your focus on virtually anything in Nature: a curling cloud, the crash of an ocean wave, the shimmer of leaves in a forest canopy, the swirl of a stream. Practices, both in Nature and in your daily routine, will interpenetrate and support each other. Your spiritual opening will deepen.

Presence Practice #3 — Simple Meditation

Normally we experience the world in an alienated and separated way. Many of the problems and issues that we face in modern life arise because of the separation and alienation from the rest of life that we hold in our awareness. One of the most important causes of contemporary alienation is separation from Nature. It is an arbitrary choice we have made to separate outer nature and inner nature. We did not suddenly emerge as individual beings separate from the rest of life. We are part of a continuum of life that has been here for at least a billion years. Every molecule, atom, and cell in your being flows back millions and millions of years as part of an interconnected whole of life.

The following two meditations are doorways to changing our tendency to separate ourselves from the rest of the world. They involve experiencing the world, and all of Nature, as one with you. These practices can bring you into a realization of the natural ecological unity that you share with the rest of life. By reconnecting with all of Nature you can dissolve fear, contraction, alienation, and separation. We have the opportunity to experience Gaia as our family. We can experience ourselves as being part of the whole family of life, which is the truth.

The first step of this exercise is a simple process that involves connecting with beings in Nature to refine presence. If you cannot go out into wild Nature, you can do this in a park, in a garden, or even in your backyard. The key is to find a place that inspires you — a place that gives you a sense of harmony, peace, and tranquility.

Next, select a being in Nature to share your practice with. There are many options for you. You can choose to connect with stones, trees, water, or clouds. I find it helpful to work with water or leaves because they are constantly in a state of movement. Because water is flowing and moving, and leaves are often shifting and changing, there is a quality of nowness that is always there with them. These are ideal partners for presence meditation.

You can do this in either a standing or sitting meditation posture. Sit or stand comfortably with that wonderful being of Nature in front of you. Let your mind focus on the way in which that being of Nature moves. Stay pristinely present without being distracted. If any thoughts or emotions come up, let them come, let them arise, and then let them go. Bring the mind gently back to that being of Nature you have chosen.

Nature is full of constant change and interconnectedness, interdependence, and intercommunion between all the beings of Nature. Delight in being part of that. If any other things arise around you, such as sound from a bird, do not look at them as distractions. Honor the presence of that occurrence in the moment. As you delight in your communion with your being of Nature, allow all other experiences of sight, sound, smell, taste, and touch to arise, manifest, and disappear as part of the background for that whole experience. Go deeper into the pure awareness of nowness. All creatures of Nature have the same pure awareness at the core of their being. You share that. They are totally present with the now, just as you are.

As you continue this process, be sure to delight in the feelings of harmony, tranquility, peace, serenity, and natural communion that arise from being interconnected with all of life. Realize that the pure awareness that underlies your form is the same pure awareness that underlies the web of life.

Simple Meditation: Stream

If you are meditating with a stream, let your mind stay completely present with the way the water is, moment to moment. Stay present as it flows, swirls, ripples, leaps, and pools. Let your mind move precisely into the form of the stream wherever your eyes rest, and stay with the form of the stream as it changes. If your mind wanders off into thoughts about how the stream just was, or what the stream might be like in a few moments, bring the mind gently back to the way the stream is in the here and now.

Simple Meditation: Leaves, Flowers, and Other Plants

Try meditating with the leaves of a tree, a flower, or a plant. Let your eyes rest exactly on the form of the plant as it is, moment to moment. Stay present with the shapes, patterns, and play of light. Let your mind remain undistracted with the beauty of that form. Feel the joy of merging at a deep level through this quality of pure presence.

*Presence Practice #4 — Connection Through
the Five Perceptual Fields*

You are in a state of continuous and constant exchange with all of Nature. Plants, flowers, animals, mountains, streams, clouds — all are your brothers, sisters, and cousins. The Native Americans say, "All the beings of Nature are all my relations." Your energy is constantly merging with Nature. Vital universal qi is given to you, and you give it back to Nature in a continuous reciprocal pattern. The boundaries between Nature and yourself are somewhat artificial. You are one with both a larger organic ecosystem and the vast body of Gaia. You know this because with every breath you take, Nature flows into you. Also, the breath that was you flows out into Nature with every exhalation that you make. When you walk barefoot on the Earth you are exchanging your energy with Mother Earth. All the food that sustains you is taken in from the outer world. When you excrete, you give back to Nature what is needed to build soil, which is the basic foundation for life on Mother Earth's surface. Through your genetic makeup and DNA, you have a profound connection all the way back to the very birth of life itself.

The perceptual fields cultivation is a way of realizing that all beings of Nature are actually your close relatives. As you deepen into this practice through each one of your senses, you will discover that you are in a state of natural union or communion with everything that arises in each field. However, for this realization to occur in an authentic way, the practices must be cultivated regularly and with heartfelt commitment.

Until this point you have been meditating with your natural relations in a general way. Now, you will refine this practice with the following five meditations. Each meditation involves refining each one of your five perceptual fields — sight, sound, taste, smell, and touch. In working with these fields of awareness, I recommend that you return to a favorite spot or find another quiet place in Nature that inspires you. In this practice you will cultivate each one of your perceptions as a way of connecting to Nature. Sit or stand in a meditation posture and relax. We will be working with each of the five senses independently. It would be good to take a few minutes before beginning the perceptual field meditation. First, bring an inner smile to your face, lips, and eyes. Feel your smiling energy. Gently smile this friendly, loving feeling down from the crown of the head to the feet, into your whole body and all its organs. Second, once the smiling down practice is complete, let the mind rest with each in-breath and out-breath for a few minutes, until the mind, body, energy, and emotions feel relaxed, focused, settled, and totally present. Then begin one or more of the following five meditations. You do not have to do all five during the same meditation period. It is fine to focus on one of these practices at a time for any given session, or for a cycle of repeated sessions, until you feel ready to move on to the next perceptual meditation. Maintain a high degree of presence with each of these perceptual field meditations.

Sound

First, close your eyes and bring your awareness into your sense of sound. Remain completely present with the precise quality of sound as it is in each moment. Surrender the past. As sounds continue arising from Nature, allow them to be experienced internally as well as noticing that they have an external cause. Do not make any separations between how the sounds arise in outer nature and how they arise within. Feel it, hear it, and experience it as an inner reality just as much as it is coming from outer nature. For example, if you hear the sound of a bird or the sound of the wind, realize that the sound is manifesting completely within as well as completely without. Notice the sound arising as one unified field—one unified experience—inside and outside, totally together. Heighten your sense of the unique nowness of each instant of sound. Rest and enjoy the experience of union of inner and outer sound.

Sight

Next, open your eyes softly and shift your consciousness to your perception of sight. Look, maintaining the whole field of vision in a calm, open, soft gaze. Again emphasize remaining completely present with exactly what is arising in your field of vision, moment by moment. Don't jump ahead to what might be seen in the unreal future. Don't dwell in sights that have just finished. Stay totally present. Allow your eyes to see with the panorama of the whole eye, not just with center-focused vision. In the beginning, it may help to emphasize the outer circle of your peripheral vision even more than the core. After practicing in that way for a while, see everything within the field of vision simultaneously and equally weighted.

As you look at your surroundings, follow that experience of vision back into yourself. Realize that whatever you see is happening just as much within inner nature, as it is in outer nature. The two are totally interconnected. Realize there is no point where what you see outside can be separated from that which you are experiencing inside. If a beautiful bird comes by, enjoy the movement of the bird within. If you see the wind moving the grass in the field, delight in the beautiful waving of the grass within the field of mind—inner and outer moving together in perfect harmony and presence. Begin to realize that everything seen is an interconnected inner-outer reality, a natural communion of your own inner nature and outer nature. By meditating in this way, you may begin to have the experience of outer nature and inner nature joining, coming into a state of communion. After a period of cultivation, you may realize the seer and the seen are always one in now.

Touch

Shift your awareness to whatever you are sensing through touch. Realize your complete connection to being in the now. No other time truly exists. Recognize the continuum of the experience of touch, however that sensation arises for you. Whatever you sense through your perceptual field of touch in the outer world of Nature, feel that it is an extension of your essence within. You have no inner or outer separation with the touch of the wind, the feel of the earth, the soft caress of the wildflowers, or the rough bark through the palms of your hands. Realize all these experiences in a state of perfect communion within and without. No separation, inside or out.

If you are sitting on a beautiful stone, experience the feeling of the stone. Let the experience of the stone's hardness move up into you. Use your awareness and perception of touch skillfully by realizing there is no separation between the points of contact with the stone externally and the experience of sitting on the stone internally.

Smell

Now shift your perception to the sense of smell. Most animals smell in a profoundly sophisticated way. You too can cultivate a more refined sense of smell. The experience of smell can be your way of deep communion, very naturally. All you have to do is let go of your ideas of separation between you and what is smelled. Once again, to really open to the magic of smell, you need to cultivate the pure instant of what is sensed. Do not be distracted by smells that have just passed or by wondering what smells still may arise.

For example, if you are embracing a beautiful tree, take a soft, deep breath through your nose. Feel the aroma of that tree fill your being. Each moment sense the perfume arising from the tree. You and your experience of this beautiful fragrance are not divided. You are not separate from the tree, and the tree is not separate from you. Rest there and bathe in that nowness.

Taste

Finally, you will cultivate the perception of taste. The living beings of Nature in your immediate environment are there to help you with this practice. Stones, water, and other inorganic beings can also assist you. Of course, be sure that whatever you taste is clean, nonpoisonous, and nonirritating. For example, you could begin by embracing a beautiful tree that has some exposed sap; then you can very lightly taste this wonderful plant ambrosia. Be sure to savor and linger with the taste. Become aware of its subtle nuances. Pay attention to how your impressions change over time. Stay in presence with each sensory sensation.

Often, I travel on foot through the mountains of my home territory in the Sangre de Cristo Mountains of southern Colorado. Many groves of aromatic ponderosa pine grace the sacred lands I call home. The smell of ponderosa pine sap is similar to a fine butterscotch candy. No matter how many contractions and distractions are crowding my mind, the fragrance of the sap and the gleam of the ponderosa's amber lifeblood always stop my world. Nothing else exists but that incredible moment. Seeing the glisten of amber sap seeping from the bark, I stop, ask permission of the tree to share its golden blood, and place a bit of blonde sap in my mouth. The explosion of its pungency stays with me for hours, slowly dissolving into my being.

If you are relating with a stone you can gently taste the stone. While you do this, feel like you are kissing your lover. Feel yourself lightly merging in union. Feel a total lack of separation between yourself and what is being tasted. Feel the magic of that instant. Everything is of one taste, not many. As the doorway to one taste opens, it also opens the door to the fundamental unity underlying yourself and all your relations in Nature.

Bringing Practice Back to Everyday Life

You can bring these perceptual field practices into your everyday life nearly anywhere and anytime. Because life in Nature is usually more relaxed, natural, and undistracted, it is good to cultivate presence in a natural environment. Once you have taken special time to cultivate each sense field in Nature, you can bring this skill right into the heart of busy, distracted city living. Presence is always there, whether you are with family or friends, at the office, or in the car. You can always cultivate presence-centered meditation of the sense fields despite whatever is going on in your life. Present-centered awareness is simply being here now. It is as simple as that.

As you return to the busyness and distractedness of your life, you will find that present-centered awareness can spontaneously arise in situations that previously might have been tense and anxious. You may find that now you can spontaneously practice presence and relaxation in many circumstances that previously made you distracted and contracted. When this new level of presence occurs, it will be a great blessing. If you continue cultivating precise presence in this way, ultimately glimpses of true mastery may arise.

Deepening Your Practice

Continually return to Nature, and when possible, return to a familiar place where you have already been practicing. By doing this, you will begin to develop specific associations with Gaia's children in that place. Developing good relationships with Nature is no different from developing good relations in the human family and community. You bring your appreciation, love, respect, and good works to your home ecosystem. You cultivate with meditation, prayer, simple heartfelt ceremony, and environmental work to protect *all* your relatives. As you deepen your practice in this way, you will move into a state of deep communion with all your organic and inorganic relations. To help you in this, continue going through the entire practice sequence with each one of the senses.

Focus your awareness completely on the experience of this practice. Allow your awareness to experience only pure presence, unity, and communion. At this level of your practice, spend as much time as you are able to but be comfortable with your commitment of time. Do not force any of these practices. There may be some things that you are not able to touch, taste, or smell. Use whatever senses are natural to you. However, if you can work with all five senses, that's wonderful. When you merge pure presence with deep relaxation, a new world opens up for you. Then the sacred view, the unity between you and all life on Mother Earth, can bloom like a flower.

After you have cultivated the perceptual field practices, you can move beyond the five senses. You can learn to cultivate the other linkages that interconnect you in an unfolding, organic ecosystem. Your emotions, thoughts, and inner feelings about all the beings of Nature also interconnect you with Gaia and your local ecosystem in a powerful way. You can also contemplate the energy that you and all forms share together. Realize that thought, life force, and emotion forge powerful bonds within any living system. By meditating on these linkages, you can expand your realization of the complete interconnectedness of all beings. This insight is a profound precursor to liberation. Coupled with this insight, your practice of presence helps you recognize the continuously changing nature of all forms. These two insights, the interconnectedness of all form, and the continuously changing nature of all form, provide a strong foundation for deepening your realization of underlying Source.

As you spend more time practicing and meditating in your special place, you may notice many beings of Nature that you have never before observed. Even more importantly, you may experience living beings of your home environment relating to you in a new and much more familiar fashion; you may even experience them relating to you in a sacred way. Birds, animals, clouds, and stones may begin to serve as holders of heart and wisdom. Gaia may arise as your teacher. At the very least, you will be able to relate to your special place in an entirely new way. A level of profound, deep connection and communion can arise with everything in that special place until the entire site merges with you in a natural, sacred mandala.[3] The secret—the true seed behind all this—is being in a state of precise, absolute, pure presence with each of these great beings of Nature. Through your cultivation all of the senses, Nature may begin to arise as the teacher of your true nature.

---

3. A geometric or pictorial design often enclosed in a circle, representing the entire universe. Mandalas can be used in meditation and ritual in Buddhism and Hinduism. In Jungian psychology, a mandala represents the self and can be a symbol of harmony within the individual.

Cultivating Universal Energy

As PRESENCE AND RELAXATION BECOME MORE FIRMLY established in your being, a natural synergy and wonderful alchemy arise. Embodying these qualities helps increase the flow of essential energy, or qi. The more present and relaxed you are, the more qi begins to flow freely, smoothly, and powerfully through your body.

Cultivating qi in Nature is a direct way to begin your path of spiritual opening through energy. Wild, unpolluted Nature holds within itself an absolutely pure, fresh, clear quality of energy, which is very difficult to find in modern human culture. Deep relaxation and presence allow you to be at one with this great current of universal energy that governs everything on Earth.

Progressively deeper levels of experience become available as you let go of mental distractions and habitual physical contractions. As you become more adept at energy cultivation, energy can be stored in your body to be used at a later time. Power gathered in this way can be used for enhancing healing, creativity, play, or meditation.

Ancient Roots

Indigenous peoples of the world have developed and preserved many ways of cultivating vitality. The roots of these energy lineages date back to the early history of these cultures. Ancient practices such as acupuncture, Qi Gong, and (more recently) T'ai Chi Ch'uan are Chinese forms of engaging with natural energy. For example, T'ai Chi Ch'uan is a martial art that cultivates qi while facilitating healing and meditative awareness. Regularly practiced over time, such indigenous practices help you cultivate powerful internal energy.

The Native Americans also had a number of Nature-centered practices for cultivating this universal power. Because the essential processes for gathering qi are fairly consistent in all cultures, it is not surprising that Native American practices are similar to those of the Chinese mystics, Indian yogis, and Tibetan Buddhist monks. As in China, enhancing qi outdoors was encouraged to help absorb the gifts of vitality that Mother Earth and Father Sky offer.

These cultures believed that developing universal energy would provide good health, thereby allowing an individual to have a long, happy life. A longer life also gave one greater opportunity for realizing liberation. In addition, daily qi cultivation provided the ancient practitioners with the ability to meditate for long periods of time. By walking barefoot, or wearing sandals made of leather or other natural fibers, they derived great energetic benefit from constant contact with the Earth, keeping them close to the flowing qi of Nature. They believed that union with Nature was a precursor to full liberation.

Clearing Energetic Blockages

A major benefit of cultivating qi is the clearing of energetic blockages. As you relax into the amplified flow of energy, blockages and obscurations that have lain dormant push to the surface to be released. This is a critical aspect of spiritual transformation. Clearing these blockages helps bring your organ systems back into balance. The harmonious flow of qi arises from opening and clearing the energy pathways of your body. These pathways are the same as the Chinese meridians and channels used in acupuncture. The proper functioning and flow of these conduits is essential to your achieving optimal health. Inserting acupuncture needles into meridians helps clear many of the energetic blockages that exist in the body. At a higher level of healing, practices such as Qi Gong or T'ai Chi work to open energetic conduits without the use of needles.

Healing Power of Qi

The self-healing benefits of qi cultivation begin by your invoking the flow of natural energy. The five foundational reasons to cultivate universal energy are achieving optimal health; increasing longevity; enabling deeper understanding of one's spiritual, emotional, and mental self; increasing joy of life by uniting with the energy that runs through the entire universe; and opening a dynamic path to ultimate liberation.

Contemporary urban settings, laden with disharmony and anxiety, are characterized by relatively unnatural energies. By contrast, Nature's life force is normally very balanced and tranquil. Therefore, by connecting with Nature energetically, you can rebalance at levels that would be difficult to accomplish otherwise. This is particularly true for those people who have lived all their lives out of contact with natural vigor and rhythm. For these unfortunates, there are no benchmarks, no standards to help point them towards the cultivation of healthy vitality. However, immersion in the natural world, combined with skillful training, can begin to open a new view.

Practicing outside allows you to connect with many different kinds of qi. For example, morning qi is the most regenerative type of universal energy. Early morning jaunts into a park or wild place are highly beneficial. The optimal time for you to cultivate universal energy in Nature is from predawn to seven or eight o'clock in the morning. The magical moment of sunrise is a very auspicious time to practice. For those of you who have begun to sense qi more deeply, you may actually begin to feel the yang qi begin stirring well before sunrise. During the morning times, outdoor energy is considered to be living qi, filled with the greatest amount of vitality, and it is extremely beneficial to life.

After midday, the energy is often called dispersing qi or relaxed qi. At this time the energy has moved into a more leisurely flow, symbolizing the process of letting go. At the close of day, it is beneficial to do moving Qi Gong, as it helps to release the obstructions and obscurations that have been built up over the day. This is also an excellent time to increase your relaxation levels—it is the period of day when your body naturally wants to relax and release your accumulated daily tensions.

Although energy cultivation practice is quite simple, it can deliver remarkable results. It opens your magical, invisible world of life force, enabling you to explore your own soul. Interactions with Nature induce restful sleep and help you wake up feeling refreshed and full of vitality. It is not necessary to understand what types of energetic gifts each tree, flower, or boulder may be bestowing. You simply need to practice regularly, be present, and be free.

An Appalachian Moment: The Spontaneous Activation of Qi

In the early 1970s I was studying with a T'ai Chi teacher from the lineage of Cheng Man-Ch'ing. I was told many miraculous stories about how universal energy could protect you from unseen enemies. We were advised never to walk up behind the master teachers in a way that might surprise them. If they were surprised, it could be dangerous because their qi would immediately activate and protect. The martial aspect of their energy cultivation could result in a violent encounter. For quite a while, I thought these were tall tales. I had never seen anything of the sort happen. I remained open to the possibility of these stories being true, yet I was still somewhat skeptical.

One day, I was alone at my farm in the Appalachian Mountain region of West Virginia. The forest surrounded me as I sat, high in a beautiful hollow. Below me the hill curved gently down among open meadows to an old apple orchard that the white-tailed deer enjoyed on their frequent forays. Behind me was a vast forest that stretched many miles back into the mountains. The entire region was filled with wildlife. Flocks of wild turkeys were abundant by day; in the evening, calls of whip-poor-wills graced the hollow with their song. Black bears, and even a few eastern panthers, were starting to return.

Evening was approaching and I was delighting in an incredibly beautiful panorama of mountains, hills, and forests. I was doing a simple Qi Gong practice in which you sit and meditate with all of Nature's elements, while keeping the mind in the tantien.[4] As the hill fell away in front of me, I felt the nurturing support of the vast forest behind. I sank into a mood of thankfulness, grateful to be alive. I could feel an accumulation of all of the

---

4. There is a basic principle in energy cultivation that says, wherever the mind goes, the qi follows. The energy follows the mind's focus. So if you direct the mind to the lower tantien, the qi goes there. If you concentrate the mind on the upper tantien point between the eyebrows, the qi goes there. If you concentrate the mind on the Laogong points in the palms of the hands, the qi will go to these points. Energy cultivation emphasizes building energy first and foremost in the lower tantien, because it can be stored there as if it were a battery.

natural energies from the mountains, forests, and plants flowing into me.

Meditating cross-legged in that beautiful spot for an hour, I suddenly felt an immense creature coming up behind me. Perhaps it was one of those panthers. I did not have time to think about what was happening. The mind's instantaneous alert and the qi took over. Because my mind was resting with the qi in the tantien, my energy activated from there. In the next split second of time, I found myself suspended six feet above the Earth in the air. Then I was spun around one hundred eighty degrees, with my arms out to the side and my palms facing forward, ready for anything. As I gently fell back to the Earth, I saw eight white-tailed deer in front of me; all had crept out of the forest.

These beautiful deer were curious about me. They had moved stealthily up behind me to a distance of about ten to fifteen feet. When I suddenly shot into the air and spun around, they all jumped, snorted, and flagged their white tails, bounding off in eight directions. It was a magnificent sight. I remained in an amazed silence.

This story illustrates how rapidly qi can activate once it is properly cultivated. Because my encounter with the deer was quite magical, it opened my mind to a whole new level of experience. I then understood how many of the great masters had naturally, without thought, been protected by their qi. Not only were the deer drawn by the practice I was doing, but they may also have contributed some of their own qi to my meditation. They left with such magnificence and grace that afterwards I felt a deep and powerful connection with the whitetail—one that I had never felt before. These insights and experiences often come in ways that are totally spontaneous, natural, and completely uncontrived.

The Gift of Love

You can offer your love and appreciation back to Nature for the energetic blessings and gifts she bestows upon you during your practice. Every time you receive a gift of qi from a plant, animal, mountain, or sacred stone, please be sure to give back your love and appreciation to Mother Earth. Honor whatever being in Nature gives you such a gift. To not show appreciation is being rather parasitic. The modern human has a tendency to do this anyway by our incessant extraction of natural resources without any expression of thanks. How many times do we consciously offer a genuine expression of gratitude from our hearts? If you give back your love and appreciation, then you become a partner. It is like giving back love to a close friend or a lover. Imagine the impact on these relationships if all you ever did was take from them and never expressed your gratitude and appreciation. Giving love back to Nature is no different from showing appreciation for a gift received from family, friends, or your lover. This uncontrived reciprocal exchange is the right kind of relationship to build with all your relations in Nature.

Cultivating Universal Energy Practice #1: Embracing the Tree Series

Every journey begins with a first step. A wonderful first step for cultivating universal energy is a sequence of exercises that come from the Chinese energy cultivation exercises known as Qi Gong. This particular progression I call the "Embracing the Tree Series." In it, I have joined together a succession of separate Qi Gongs into one unified sequence of positions. This progression allows you to hold the entire cycle of postures much longer than if you were to attempt to hold only one stance without changing. Also, this particular combination of standing Qi Gongs has a much more beneficial effect when done together, than if you were to practice only one of the positions alone.

The ancient Taoists spent years in the mountains perfecting these Qi Gong practices by watching inner and outer nature very closely. Because they loved Nature, they connected deeply with trees, animals, and all the elements. They cultivated an intimate relationship with wood, fire, earth, metal, and water. I believe the individual Qi Gongs in this series originated when these ancient people communed with trees in profound ways. Through this practice they discovered many secrets of energetic renewal.

You can practice the embracing the tree Qi Gong by encircling your arms around an actual tree, or simply by envisioning one. You can also just choose to practice in the presence of nearby trees you would like to share with. Because you can visualize the tree, you can practice this Qi Gong anywhere, anyplace, and anytime. However, the best results are achieved in Nature where there is a lot of qi, especially qi coming from the plants and trees. As with the ancient Taoists, be sure to develop a good heart connection and cultivate deep appreciation with any tree that agrees to share itself with you.

Preparation and Posture Guidelines

Embracing the tree Qi Gong is a standing meditation practice. During this practice you will be moving through a series of different arm positions. This practice, as well as all energy cultivation practices, should be performed with leather or cotton-soled shoes. If it is warm enough, simply go barefoot. As I mentioned previously, this allows a direct energy connection with Mother Earth, particularly through the kidney points (K1) in your feet. Rubber soles create an energetic barrier and insulate you, to some degree, from the energy that the Earth has to offer.

- To begin, stand with your feet directly under your hips. A straight line from the hip joint would penetrate through the center of your foot.

- Your knees are slightly relaxed in an unlocked position.

- Toes are pointing straight ahead, or, for women, they can be slightly toed out.

- The lower back is relaxed. Release any excessive curve to the lower back and coccyx.

- The pelvic girdle is naturally dropped and relaxed. Relaxing the lower back and pelvis may provide the sensation that your pelvis is tucking slightly forward from the base. Feel your pelvis sinking from the lower abdomen all the way down through the legs down into the Earth. You can achieve this feeling by releasing any muscular tension in the abdominal region as well as in the lower back area.

- Visualize the thread of your spirit lifting into Heaven from the crown of your head. Consistent with the meridian system, the actual location is the Bai Hui or Hundred Meetings point. As the thread of spirit lifts you into the sky, you are also sinking down into the Earth with your lower body. This combination of simultaneous lifting and sinking forces also separates the vertebrae of your spine. There is the sensation of plenty of space for each vertebra to function. Once again, lift skyward and simultaneously gently allow the sternum and upper body to relax and settle slightly downward.

- Review your posture by feeling your feet embracing the Earth. Focus on the forward center of the sole of each foot—this spot is called the Bubbling Spring point, or the kidney 1 point. It is located slightly behind the padding where the big toe and the other four toes meet in the center of the front one-third of each foot. This Bubbling Spring point is a spot where you can make a profound connection with Mother Earth. Send your love to her through this connection point, and in exchange receive her vitality. This is also the point from which you can kiss Gaia as you walk. Allow the entire foot to spread out and embrace Mother Earth.

- Bring your entire body into alignment. Make sure your head and neck are placed with the ears directly above the shoulders. Your chin is horizontal with the Earth.

- This posture now allows energy to circulate naturally up, parallel to your spine, over the crown of the head, and back down the front centerline of your body, which is the natural circulation pattern for your vital energy.

Breathing Instructions

- Establish deep, natural breathing into the lower abdomen with no tension in the diaphragm. You want your breath to be soft, smooth, deep, gentle, and fine. Your breathing should not be forced in any way. Also, feel the sides and lower back of your lower torso expand a bit with each in-breath and subside slightly with each out-breath.

- Place the tip of your tongue behind your upper front teeth. (You can gradually progress to placing the tip of the tongue on the roof of the palate once you become com-

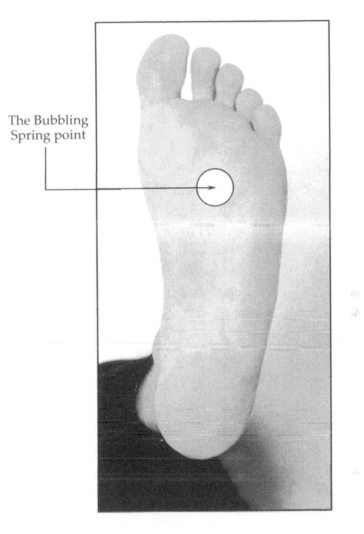

The Bubbling
Spring point

fortable with the placement behind the upper front teeth. Again, the guiding principle is to be able to do so in a relaxed fashion.)

Soft Gazing

- Keep the eyes open. Relax any tension around the eyes and forehead. Direct the eyes slightly downward at an angle of forty-five degrees. Take in the entire field of vision rather than looking at a single point. When you softly gaze with your eye's entire view, you see the world as a whole interconnected field. By doing so, you are actually creating wholeness within you.

- Do a brief body scan, with smiling and relaxed energy, to make sure that you are not holding any excess tension anywhere in the body; be sure that you are really deeply relaxed before you begin this practice.

- If you experience any tingling sensations in your body as you do any of these Qi Gongs, it is normally a good sign—it means that your vital energy is beginning to flow.

Position # 1—Embracing the Tree

Lift your arms in front of you into a circular shape as if you were holding a great sphere or were embracing a beautiful tree. Your arms are at the height of your heart and thymus gland. Your thumbs and fingers face each other, with six to eight inches between the fingertips of your hands. As you hold the arms out, totally relax your shoulders. Feel the heaviness of the elbows. Allow the elbows and arms to release any tension through their heaviness.

While the shoulders, arms, and elbows are relaxed, the hands and the wrists have lightness to them and feel like they are effortlessly floating. You will feel an energetic connection between the fingertips of each hand when you move them into a truly connected position.

Experiment with Qi Flow

Hold this position for at least five minutes. Experiment by keeping the left hand completely still; then move the right hand a little bit, as if you were waving it slightly. As you wave the right hand back and forth across the extended fingers of the left hand, you should be able to feel a tingling sensation. A shifting of the circulation of the qi between the left arm and the right arm causes that tingling. The left arm tends to be more receptive—it is the yin arm; the right arm tends to be more active—it is the yang arm. As

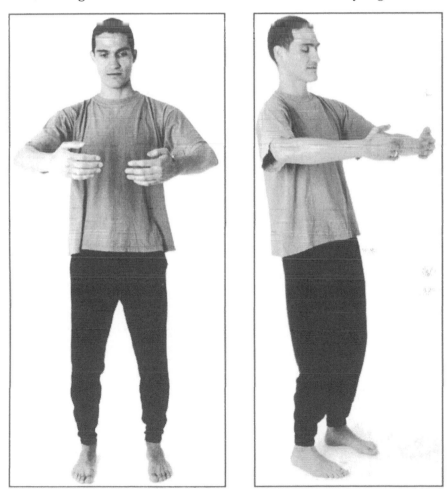

Embracing the tree posture

you wave your right hand, you are playing with your energy circulation.

Now, return to the original posture with your arms making a circular form, palms facing your heart. If you feel tension, anxiety, or strain, gently let your awareness move into that part of your body and release it. Let the tension go. Let it relax. Let all the stress sink down through your body, down through the soles of your feet. Give this stress to Mother Earth; she can absorb and transmute any kind of tension or negativity. She transforms all of our tension, toxic waste, and negative by-products into beautiful soil.

Position #2 — Embracing the Buddha Belly

After you have held Position #1 for about five minutes, gently bring your arms down, still maintaining a rounded shape. When in this posture, feel like you are holding a great, giant, laughing Buddha's belly. Slowly bring your arms down until the centers of your palms are six to eight inches apart, palms facing inwards toward the lower tantien. The palms are considered to be major energy centers, called the Laogong (the work palace) points. Feel the universal energy accumulating. Feel a natural connection between the centers of your palms and the tantien.

At the beginning of your practice, the tantien energy center will be small. However, as you continue to cultivate your energy, the tantien expands and becomes larger. It is best to locate the tantien before you begin the exercise. This will enable you to naturally move your arms from the embracing the tree position into this embracing the Buddha belly posture. Hold this Qi Gong for about five minutes. This is a much easier posture to hold than the embracing the tree position, so it may be easier for you to relax. If there are any tensions that you could not release in the first posture, you should be able to release them in this pose. This Qi Gong allows you to safely store additional qi in your lower tantien, especially if you rest your mind in the tantien while cultivating it.

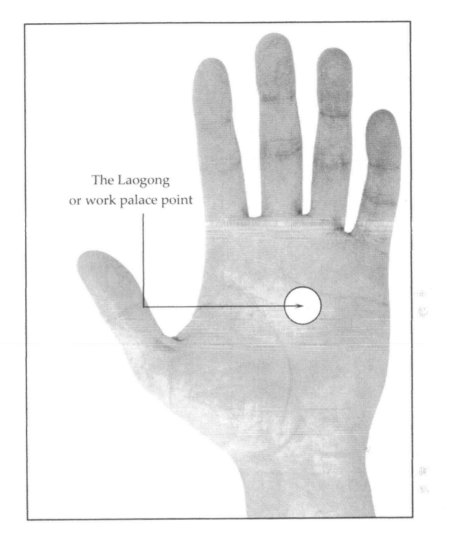

The Laogong
or work palace point

Position #3—Thumbs Up, Accentuate the Positive

After five minutes, let the arms lift up again so that the palm centers are facing the heart one more time. Revisit all the principles for the posture as before. Consciously relax the whole body, legs, feet, head, and shoulders. This time, lift the thumbs straight up so that they are pointing toward the sky. It may be helpful to imagine your thumbs as antennae that bring in the energy of the cosmos. As you keep your thumbs up, rotate the palms slightly outward

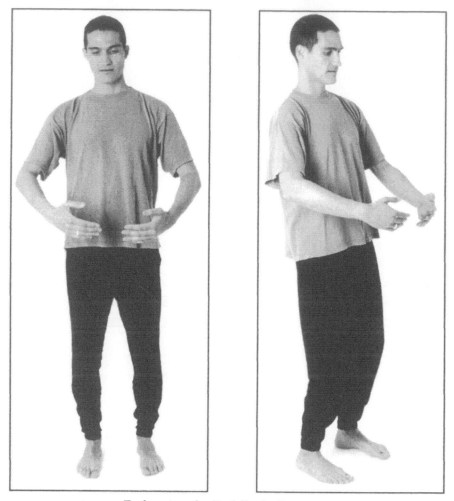

Embracing the Buddha belly posture

from the index fingers. Your fingertips are still facing each other about six to eight inches apart. This minimal turning of the palms will circulate the energy in a slightly higher orbit.

This posture will help activate the circulation of energy from the lower and middle sections of your back, all the way up over the crown of the head, and back down the front of the body. This pat-

100

tern of energy circulation is part of what is called "the microcosmic orbit" in the Chinese Taoist system.

Hold Position #3 for about five minutes. While in this position, gently pay attention to the circulation of energy between the fingers. Bring your awareness to the accumulation of qi in the tantien, and allow yourself to feel a beautiful connection with Mother Earth through the soles of your feet. Feel the wonderful connection with Father Sky through the crown of your head. Feel the connection with all the plants and the animals surrounding you. Feel all of Nature naturally interconnecting and exchanging universal energy with you.

At this point, let your arms drop and return to the embracing the Buddha belly, Position #2. Hold it again for about five minutes. As you systematically move from each of the upper arm positions in the embracing the tree series, the embracing the Buddha belly position is used as an intermediary posture to help the arms and upper body relax and to store the qi accumulated by the lifted-arm Qi Gongs.

Position #4—Embracing Heaven and Cultivating the Upper Tantien

After you have held the embracing the Buddha belly position for five minutes, face away from the Sun. Lift your arms up in front of you a foot or so higher than your head level. Relax. Keep the circular form of the arms, and again keep the fingertips six to eight inches apart, relating to the hand-to-hand energy flow. Relax the shoulders. Relax the arms. Face the Laogong points in each palm center toward a point located between your eyebrows—your upper tantien. Visualize a qi connection between each Laogong point and your upper tantien.

If possible, gaze out into the sky in front of you between the fingertips; then feel the sky qi flowing back into your eyes, hands, arms, and upper tantien. If looking into the sky is too hard on your eyes, close them as you do the Qi Gong, but look up toward and into your upper tantien from behind closed eyelids. Feel the sky qi flowing into you as before.

Once again, at the conclusion of embracing Heaven and cultivating the upper tantien, let your arms drop and return to the embracing the Buddha belly, Position #2. Hold it yet again for about five minutes. Let the arms and upper body relax, and store the qi accumulated by the lifted-arm Qi Gong.

Because this upper tantien cultivation can tend to leave you feeling ungrounded, it is very important to do the embracing the Buddha belly Qi Gong until you feel fully grounded again. It also helps you to feel a very deep Earth connection as you do this practice. In particular, feel your roots going deep down into subterranean Gaia from your Bubbling Spring points. Feel your own qi and Gaia's qi joining in your lower tantien—grounding you.

Position #5—Embracing the Three Spheres

After you have held embracing the Buddha belly position for five minutes, lift your arms up to your heart level again. Relax. This will be the final position, which is called "embracing the three spheres." This time, as you lift your arms up, bring your hands into a position as if you are wrapping your fingers around a delicious grapefruit (a sphere about four to six inches in diameter). Keep the fingertips and thumbs of each hand about an inch apart from each other. Imagine creating, at heart height, a level platform with your index fingers and thumbs that could support a small plate in a horizontal position. The other three fingers can splay out and wrap around the imaginary ball. Keep a bit of tension in the fingers, imagining that they are encircling this imaginary sphere, but keep the rest of the body relaxed.

Now, imagine holding a second, larger sphere with your arms that presses against your chest and the insides of your arms. Keep some tension in the arms as you hold this ball so that it is secure. You are now holding two balls: a small one, held with your hands, and a larger one, held by your arms. There should be a little con-

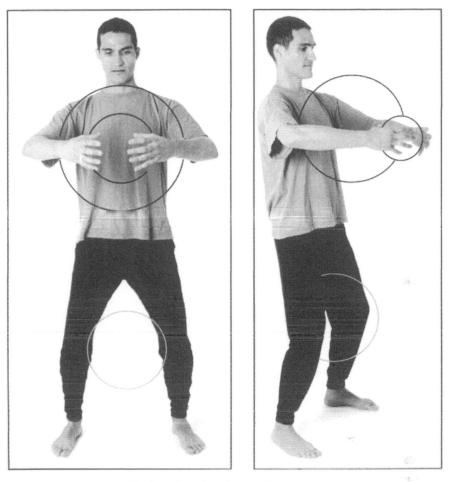

Embracing the three spheres posture

scious tension in both hands and arms to hold these spheres, but relax everything else not related to holding the spheres.

Finally, add the feeling of a third imaginary sphere. This one you are holding between your thighs, knees, and lower legs. Squeeze this third sphere gently between your thighs.

There should be three areas of tension—one between the fingers and the hands, another between the arms, and the third

103

between the thighs and knees. The rest of the body is positioned as
before and is completely relaxed.

Place your attention on the lower tantien. Through your
awareness, bring the connection with Mother Earth and the link
with Father Sky to your tantien. Feel the external qi flowing into
you, adding to your store of postnatal qi. If you need to shift your
attention to the three points of light tension where you are holding
the spheres, gently move it from one point to the next. If possible,
try to maintain some of your attention in the lower tantien at all
times. Hold Position #4 for five minutes. You will most likely find
that this posture effectively builds energy. You may feel a lot of tingling or other energy sensations as you do this.

Concluding the Embracing the Tree Series

To finish the embracing the tree series, naturally let the arms
relax back into the original Position #1 momentarily. Then conclude with the embracing the Buddha belly, Position #3, allowing
the energy to naturally accumulate in the lower tantien area. As
you let your arms fall, straighten the body and stand relaxed and
erect. Feel the energy, vitality, and freshness. Notice your interconnectedness with all of Nature. Feel the exquisite and delicate qi
flowing into you from the trees, plants, stones, water, Sun, Mother
Earth, and Father Sky. Wherever you have been practicing, universal energy has merged with you. You feel refreshed and regenerated.

A Special Note about Tension, Pain and Length of Practice

When you start practicing energy cultivation, you often build
up a lot of tension in the upper body. When I created this sequence,
I wanted to be sure that practitioners have the ability to relax the
upper torso completely. Five minutes in each of these postures is
just about right when you are starting out. As you develop facility,
you can go longer and longer. Many of my students do this practice for up to two hours. However, I do not recommend practicing

for more than a few minutes at a time for beginning students. Just start easy and be gentle with yourself. Do not push or overextend yourself. Utilize only seventy percent of what you feel is your full capacity. This instruction is especially important for athletes accustomed to conventional workouts in which you force your body and condition your mind to break through physical barriers and thresholds. That approach is counterproductive, even dangerous, with these exercises. While doing the embracing the tree series, if you encounter any undue strain, relax. Stop the moment you notice any pain or any sharpness from your effort. Relax and stay present.

A Variation to Play With

As you are doing this series of embracing the tree positions, you can do an initial sequence as a way of relaxing and opening. Then do another sequence to purify, and then a third sequence to regenerate and build a reservoir of qi in the lower tantien. Some people like to add a fourth sequence to emphasize proper qi circulation through their whole being. When you first begin practicing this series, however, one sequence is plenty. Remember not to force this process of qi cultivation.

If you wish to further relax and de-contract from all the holding, practice one or more of the bear Qi Gongs for a while as your conclusion. The bear Qi Gongs are an excellent way to de-contract tense muscles and tendons, and to help smooth out your qi flow after long holding sessions of Qi Gong.

This embracing the tree cycle of practices is a simple, powerful way to enhance your fundamental vitality. It will help you connect energetically with Mother Earth and Great Spirit in a profound, nurturing, purifying, and regenerating way. It will also teach you about relaxing. Qi Gongs are practices you can do for your whole life. They will bring you tremendous benefits at every level.

For optimum results, practice outside in Nature, in a fresh environment where there is no air pollution. Also, be sure to pick a place where there is minimal psychic or emotional pollution. This is particularly important because you are absorbing the qi from your environment. If you do this practice in a place that is crowded, noisy, and polluted, you will not absorb pure, vital energy.

Locating the Bai Hui Point

Hold your left hand above your head an inch or two and pass it back and forth slightly above the physical surface of the top of the back half of your head. You may feel a slight tingling point above the crown of the head in the palm of your left hand. This point is located in the central forward portion of the back half of the crown. For those who are less energy sensitive, place the thumb of your left hand between your eyebrows and extend your middle finger to the top of your head. Place the thumb of your right hand at the base of the skull, posterior to the occipital lobe of the brain, where the spine enters the skull, and similarly extend the middle finger of the right hand toward the top of the head. The Bai Hui point is located at or very near the location your two fingers meet.

Locating the Lower Tantien

Over the years, I've developed the following technique to help people locate their lower tantien. You can find the precise location of your lower abdominal energy center by taking the three middle fingers of one hand and then stacking the three fingers vertically. Start with placing the index finger at the lower edge of your belly button. Stack your middle finger below that, vertically. Then stack your fourth, ring finger below the third. Press in at the point where your fourth finger rests on your abdomen, and feel into a point about one-third of the way into your abdomen. When you press into your abdomen with the fourth finger, you can sense a place about a third of the way into your body. This is the location of the lower tantien. Keep your mind there and slowly let go of the index

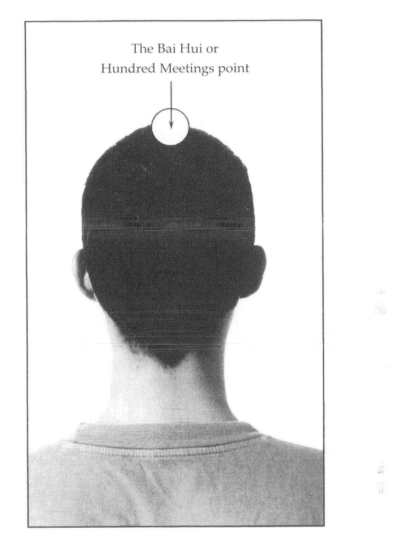

The Bai Hui or
Hundred Meetings point

and middle fingers. When your mind is stable and centered at your tantien point, slowly release your fourth finger, while keeping your mind in the tantien.

Cultivating Universal Energy Practice #2: Reciprocal Breathing

When you are relaxed and present with the magnificent essence of Nature, the plants, the exquisite beauty of a lichen-covered rock and trees, and the sweetness of fresh air, you become saturated with remarkable gifts. Recall the times when you have received an infusion of the energy from a flower by simply inhaling its aromatic essence. You can do this with any natural being or object. You can even connect with the wonderful mystery of a stone. Simply relax, ask permission, and allow yourself to be present and receive the universal energy and wisdom stored within the stone. To our Native American elders, stones are the wisdom keepers, beings holding some of this planet's most primordial acumen.

The more you enter into this interactive relationship with Nature, the more you are available to receive her many blessings. You develop the capacity to share with the environment through your love and appreciation for the true essence of everything that surrounds you. Actually, the life force that flows through you is the same living energy that runs through all of life. Likewise, the vastness of Source awareness that underlies your own being is the same Source that underlies all being. Thus, the first principle, relaxation, allows space for presence (the second principle). Relaxation and presence, when merged in the moment, allow for the cultivation of universal energy (third principle). The dynamic merging of these three qualities is often a necessary precondition for connecting with Source.

Reciprocal breathing is one of my favorite practices to join in energetic communion with Nature. I began doing this practice spontaneously as a child and it has grown and evolved for me over the years. It may be helpful to know that in many cultures, China in particular, breath is synonymous with qi. Breath is viewed as one and the same with life force. I usually describe this practice as reciprocal energy breathing, or reciprocal exchange of energy, with the qi riding the breath. This cultivation can help you experience profound connectedness. There is a very simple way to do it, very similar to how I usually did it as a child. There is also a more sophisticated approach that I developed several decades ago. Both practices have been a source of great joy and energetic renewal for me. I will share both of these methods with you below.

Starting with Trees

The simplest approach to reciprocal breathing practice is to go into a natural spot and find a tree. Perhaps you could even experiment with having the precise tree choose you. Ask which tree would like to commune with you. Then truly listen with your whole being. Open yourself to feeling which tree would like to develop a relationship and then honor that feeling. Later on, one can develop reciprocal breathing relationships with flowers, a stone, or many other beings in Nature. The beings you practice with don't have to be organic to be sentient. However, initially, I would recommend starting with a tree for two reasons—trees have a special relationship with humans in the cultivation of life energy and usually these wonderful beings truly appreciate our communion with them.

Later on, you can take these same approaches you utilize for reciprocal breathing with trees and apply them to any other fellow traveler of Nature, including elemental beings such as stones, mountains, streams, clouds, Mother Ocean, and the Sun and Moon.

Once you have located a tree that would like to share energy with you, follow these basic guidelines:

- Always approach a tree respectful of its life experience. You should feel deep gratitude and appreciation for the exchange of air that you and trees perform for one another. The tree breathes in the carbon dioxide you exhale, purifying and utilizing these elements; then the tree breathes back to you the oxygen you need to live. In this intimate exchange of breath, the tree is totally present with you.

• When you go into Nature, before you begin any practice of exchange with any being of Nature, it is extremely important to ask permission. When you ask the tree if it would like to share with you, be prepared to listen. We humans have a basic assumption that Nature is just there, waiting to give us whatever we want. Gaia does not work that way. Check in and see if the living being is willing to work with you and intuitively sense whether you have been accepted or not. Sometimes it is not appropriate. This may be awkward for you at first, because we so often operate from our belief that Nature is always there to give us everything we want, wherever and whenever we want it. In these difficult times, when Nature is experiencing so much harm from humans, it is essential that we all cut through that egocentric arrogance at the root of so much of our damage to Gaia. It is especially important to realize this because humans have abused Nature for so long and in so many ways.

Listening with Your Heart

When you go into Nature and want to set a tent down, you need to ask permission of the spirits and beings of the place; for example, "Is this the right spot for the tent, or should it be somewhere else?" Pay attention to what the response from Nature and Spirit actually is. When you ask the question, ask from a quiet place in your heart and patiently wait for a reply. If it is not the right spot, you will usually feel kind of a chill or a contractedness come into you. If it is the right location, you will usually feel warmth and an opening in your heart and in your awareness. A kind of welcoming sensation arises within you.

It works the same with plants, trees, flowers, and stone people and with all the other beings of Nature. When you go to them and want to do a practice, or just be around them, it is very good to ask permission to be in their presence and to come into a deeper relationship. Sometimes the response to your request may be "no." There are times when you are at home and you turn off the phone, or you do not answer the doorbell. You would like to have some private time. It is no different with all your relatives in Nature, so respect that. All this simply means that you have to develop some sensitivity.

When you begin to become sensitive in this way, you will notice it is perfectly understandable that a lot of suspicion exists among natural beings regarding the activities and motivations of humans. If you honestly and genuinely ask permission to enter into a deeper relationship with Nature, you will be astounded by how much appreciation, joy, and thanks you receive in return for being a caring human.

All you need to do is authentically open yourself up to this kind of relationship. Do not just go into Nature assuming that you are calling all the shots. We are not in control, although we like to think we are.

Making Contact

Once you have established this new kind of relationship, you are ready to begin. Having received from your wonderful tree a response of, "Yes, I would love to enter into this cultivation practice with you," you can truly embrace the tree.

There are several ways for you to embrace the tree. You can place your hands close to the tree, facing it—you do not have to touch it—you can just touch the energy field. Or, if you wish, you can connect directly with the physical tree itself and make contact with its bark. Some people like to embrace a tree with a full hug and others like to just place their palms on the tree with their body a little bit away from the tree; others prefer to embrace the energy aura of the tree. Whatever feels right to the tree and you is fine.

- First, relax and stay present. Breathe out and radiate your love and appreciation to the tree. Admire the feel of its bark, the strength of the trunk, its deep-rooted-ness, the aroma of its sap. Clarify and sharpen all your perceptions. Utilize each perception as a bridge of communion that deepens your appreciation.

- As you take your first in-breath, feel all the gifts your tree has to give you energetically. Feel its energy flowing in through your palms and arms, and also into your lower tantien (field of the elixir). The power also flows into the middle tantien, which is located in your chest, and streams within the upper tantien, which is located between the eyebrows in your forehead. Feel the qi pouring into you from that great tree.

- Do not force your breathing. Just naturally take in whatever that great being has to give you and breathe back love and appreciation. The breath is the vehicle of the qi; life force and breath are completely interconnected and intertwined. By doing this practice, there is a beautiful reciprocal exchange of love, appreciation, and qi. This process can purify, revitalize, and regenerate you at a deep level. A simple practice like this can become profound.

- Remain there for at least five minutes, naturally exchanging back and forth. Stay as long as you and the tree remain comfortably connected. Should you receive a feeling that the tree is ready to disconnect, honor that insight. Otherwise, continue the cultivation.

- When you and the tree feel full and complete, gently breathe from your heart to the tree the love and appreciation that you feel for the gifts your tree has generously given you.

- When you bring the practice to an end, thank the tree for its time of sharing with you and gently disengage.

- Be kind and caring in the beginning; start this practice gently. Do not force it.

Your relationship with one tree can open you up to relationships with many other trees. This practice can expand your relationship with the whole Earth because your tree is connected to the entire web of life. Like you, at the deepest level, the tree arises and manifests naturally in pure Source awareness; therefore, your energetic exchange can carry you into profound union in a manner that allows you to share the mystery of pure Source awareness itself. I will offer you more insights about Source in a later chapter.

Advanced Reciprocal Breathing

If you would like to take this practice to another level, here is a wonderful way to deepen the exercise. You may choose to work with a flower, a stone, the Sun, the Moon, or any other being of Nature. However, for these instructions we will continue using the example of a tree.

- Begin, as before, by allowing yourself to be drawn to a tree. Ask its permission to exchange energies, and embrace it when you feel you have been invited to do so.

- First, breathe out your appreciation and love to the tree as in the earlier practice.

- Next, breathe in. During the in-breath, visualize heavenly qi coming down from the sky into the leaves and branches of the tree. See it pouring from the tips of the branches into the trunk. Also on the in-breath, visualize Mother Earth's sweet energy flowing up through the roots of the tree into the trunk. The tree is infused with heavenly and earthly energy, flowing into it simultaneously from above and below.

- Continuing with your same in-breath, feel the fresh combined Heaven and Earth qi flowing out through the tree's trunk into your body—particularly into your palms, arms, and torso. Feel the flow, particularly where you are in contact with the tree. If you are at some distance from the tree, feel the qi flow into all your energy meridians, channels, chakras, and three tantiens. The energy flows into you and fills your whole being. Heaven and Earth qi merge in you.

- While on the same in-breath, the energy lifts up from your crown into the sky as a gift back to Father Sky. The qi also flows down through the soles of your feet, particularly the Bubbling Spring points, to merge with Mother Earth.

- Rest for a moment, or for several breaths, and then begin cultivating with your out-breath.

- When you breathe out, you will create the same visualization as before with the in-breath, but in reverse order.

- As you initiate your in-breath, feel the Heaven qi pour down into the crown of your head from the sky above, while Earth qi rises into your feet from below. These merged energies flow into you, revitalizing and renewing you. Some of the qi continues to flow through you into the tree as a gift of appreciation from your heart. Emphasize the flow of loving energy through your palms, your heart, and your three tantiens.

- While on your same out-breath, some of the qi rises up the tree trunk through the crown of the tree and into the sky; simultaneously, some of the qi flows down through the roots into Mother Earth below.

- Upon completing the out-breath phase, rest for a breath or two, then continue with directly cultivating the practice on the in-breath, visualizing as before, the Heaven qi coming down into the tree's crown from above, and the Earth qi rising up from below into the tree's roots. Again, continuing with the in-breath, experience the energy filling the tree, flowing into you, revitalizing you, and then see the remaining qi flow up into the sky from your crown and down into Mother Earth through your feet, completing your in-breath.

- This energetic connection becomes a gift of your love and appreciation, not just to the tree, but also to Father Sky and down into Mother Earth below. You and the tree become a unified vehicle for that offering.

- During your practice, go back and forth in this way, feeling the natural exchange of love, appreciation, and primordial qi. You can gradually build up to a period of time lasting as long as forty minutes, a typical period of time for meditative sessions.

- Continue cultivating your communion with the tree through this reciprocal breathing practice for as long as it is comfortable for you and the tree.

- When you bring either of the two reciprocal breathing practices to an end, thank the tree for its time of sharing with you and gently disengage. Ground yourself by sensing your Earth connection through your Bubbling Spring points, and by centering for a few minutes in your lower tantien to conclude.

A Word of Caution

This energy work is powerful and sometimes there is a tendency for people to go to extremes. So, I find it appropriate to enter a word of caution. Because so much bliss is produced by these practices, they can become quite seductive. As you cultivate, slowly expand your capacity. Relax and be gentle with yourself and all your relations in Nature. If you do it in this way, the cultivation process will become firmly rooted in you. Your relationship to all the beings of Nature will open in a way that will astonish you. If you force it, you may frighten, even damage, the very beings of Nature you wish to honor.

Cultivating Universal Energy Practice #3: The Flashing Practice

This practice is similar to reciprocal breathing, which I call flashing. I developed this practice during my time in the Canadian Arctic and the Brooks Range of Alaska, where contact with large animals happened for me almost every day. It allowed me to make deep contact with birds and animals that were at a distance, like grizzly bears, where too close contact could have been challenging.

Flashing is a practice of gently sending energy to a bird or an animal, then remaining open to what is returned. Because birds and animals are often moving, flashing is an easier practice to accomplish with them than reciprocal breathing, which works best with more stable beings of Nature. The practice is extraordinarily simple.

- As with reciprocal breathing, first ask permission of the bird or animal to share in this cultivation. Listen. If the answer is "No," respect that. If the answer is "Yes," continue.

- When the bird or animal comes near, envision a soft, radiant, golden light emerging from your heart. See this gentle, radiant, golden light embracing the bird or animal.

- Compassionately enfold that animal with soft, loving qi. Imagine you are embracing it with affectionate energy. Remain at a distance.

- Be open and appreciate whatever is returned energetically or totemically.

It is important to be gentle as you begin this practice. Most birds and animals are so sensitive that if you do this in a strong way, it is perceived as extremely aggressive. Because it is so unusual for a modern human being to share energy in this way, you could unintentionally frighten them. So send your love and appreciation in a very soft, kind fashion.

As you gently send your bird and animal relatives loving human kindness, you may be amazed by the response. Send this kindness smoothly from your whole being and you will both send and receive extraordinary gifts.

Cultivating Universal Energy Practice #4: Purifying and Renewing the Five Yin Organs

There is extensive material related to the Chinese five element system that is beyond the scope of this book. However, it is helpful to have some awareness of this vital body of knowledge. In the classical Taoist view, your body, your energy, your emotions, and even your thoughts are connected to these five fundamental processes.

In the Taoist tradition, it is said that universal energy is stored in the three tantiens—the lower tantien, the middle tantien (chest), and the upper tantien (between the eyebrows in the vicinity of the third eye). Other storage areas include the five yin organs, the bone marrow, and the eight extraordinary meridians.

The qi is stored in the five yin organs of the body, including the liver, the heart, the spleen, the lungs, and the kidneys. Each of these five organs is associated with different elements and processes of Nature. They also have yang organ counterparts; for example, the liver is a yin organ and its counterpart, the gall bladder, is a yang organ; for the heart, the small intestine; for the spleen, the stomach; for the lungs, the large intestine; and for the kidneys, the bladder. Taken together, the Taoists view these ten organs to be the inner five gods and goddesses that make our being possible. For that reason alone, the ten inner gods and goddesses are honored daily. Remember, however, that it is only the yin organs that can actually store qi.

The essence of this practice is to visualize the associated element colors being breathed in, purifying, and then regenerating each organ system. You can then follow by toning each of the healing sounds to vibrate the appropriate organ and deepen its regeneration. The following list is the five yin and yang organ systems and their associated elements (processes)—colors and healing sounds.

- The liver and gall bladder are connected to the wood element and resonate with the color leafy green. The healing sound is pronounced "ssshhuuuw."

- The heart and small intestine are connected to the fire element and are associated with the color fiery red. The healing sound is "hhawww."

- The spleen/pancreas and stomach are connected to the earth element and are associated with an earthy yellow or golden-yellow color. The healing sound is "whhooo."

- The lungs and large intestine are connected to the metal element and resonate with a white or platinum silver color. The healing sound is "seeeaaahh."

- The kidneys and bladder are connected to the water element and are associated with the color blue-black, indigo, or even black itself, like a deep ocean. The healing sound is a nasal "sshhurrreee."

- I usually recommend finishing any work with these healing colors and sounds with visualization for the triple warmer, also referred as the triple heater or triple burner.[5] Although this regulatory function is not an organ in Western medicine, it is treated as an important organ-like regulator of particularly the yang fire functions. The colors used are white with all the rainbow colors. The healing sound you tone is "seeeeeeeee."

---

5. The triple burners are associated with the element of fire. They include yang channels from the hands to the head, and then to the pericardium. The three burners wrap in a spiral around the pericardium. The burners regulate the digestion and harmonization of food and liquids throughout the body.

119

As with many of the other cultivations, this practice can be done in a sitting, standing, or lying down meditation posture. Be sure to relax, settle the mind and emotions, and develop a naturally focused mind. In Taoism, the practice is called "the generation cycle," since each of the elements helps to nurture the next element in the sequence. Wood, for example, naturally feeds (or generates) fire.

- Starting with the wood element, visualize and breathe in a vibrant, leafy green color into your liver and gallbladder. Feel it purify these organs on your in-breath. Then exhale, breathing out all of the illnesses and blockages. Repeat nine times. The first four breaths aid in purification and the last five breaths emphasize regeneration.

- Next in sequence is the fire element. Visualize and breathe in a fiery red color into your heart and small intestine. Feel it purify these organs on your in-breath. Then, exhale, breathing out all of their illnesses and blockages. Repeat nine times.

- Next is the earth element. Visualize and breathe in an earthy yellow or golden yellow color into the spleen/pancreas and stomach. Feel it purify these organs on your in-breath. Then, exhale, breathing out all of their illnesses and blockages. Repeat nine times.

- The following element in this cycle is metal. Visualize and breathe in a white or platinum silver color into the lungs and large intestine. Feel it purify these organs on your in-breath. Then, exhale, breathing out all of their illnesses and blockages. Repeat nine times.

- The final element in this sequence is the water element. Visualize and breathe in a deep, blue-black, indigo, or even a black color like a deep ocean, into the kidneys and bladder. Feel it purify these organs on your in-breath. Then, exhale, breathing out all of their illnesses and blockages. Repeat nine times.

Once you have finished with the colors, then you can repeat the purifying and renewing sequences for each organ/element now using its unique sound. I have found toning these sounds to be most beneficial, but it is also possible to sound these internally in the mind's ear. In any case, be sure to feel the associated organ being vibrated by the sound. Again using the example of the wood element and the liver and gall bladder, you would tone nine times "ssshhuuuw."

When cultivating this five element process, it is very important that you do all six of the practices in sequence. By doing all six each time you cultivate, you maintain balance, harmony, and integration in all your organ and energy systems. If you were to do only one or two of these color and sound practices, it could lead to imbalances in your system.

Your five yin and yang organ systems actually have powerful associations with all of Nature. For example, if you are making a strong connection with a tree, then it is very natural to be able to store that energy, the wood element, in the liver. Visualizing a leafy green color when cultivating the wood element helps deepen both the practice and the connection to the tree.

When you do this five element practice, another result is deepening your communion with all of Nature's elemental processes. Remember, however, to prevent building up an excess amount of energy in any one of your organs. It is not a good idea to accumulate more qi in only one organ. For that reason, I recommend going through the entire generation cycle of all six colors and sounds to maintain balance and harmony among all the organ systems.

There is another cycle that helps reduce the amount of energy in each of the elements and in the five yin and yang organ systems. When you get to this level of refinement, please consult or connect with an experienced and knowledgeable five element process practitioner. That practitioner can give you personal advice regarding which elements need possible reduction, increase, or balancing in your system. Over time, you can move with all these practices, and also with expert support, into deeper and deeper levels of sophistication and refinement of your natural elemental processes.

Cultivating Universal Energy Practice #5: Washing the Marrow

The bone marrow is another area where you can store qi from Nature and the cosmos. Bones, bone marrow, and joints are actually some of the major storage systems for energy in the human body. It may be a little unusual for you to think of the bone marrow playing such a vital role in your being; however, Western medical science actually supports this view. We know that the blood in your body is produced in the bone marrow and that with aging your marrow changes color and becomes fatty, making your bones brittle. In the Chinese medical system, it is understood that the blood and qi share an intimate relationship. It was this understanding that led to the creation of marrow washing exercises. In our culture, we do very few things to really nurture bone marrow vitality; we are usually not even aware of its significance to our health and well-being.

The following exercise is a two-part cultivation that I created by combining two different practices from the Taoist tradition. The first part of the cultivation is used for cleansing the bone marrow. The second part is for accumulating qi in the bone marrow. When done in sequence, they form a potent healing practice for purifying and regenerating your entire energy system.

Purifying Energy in the Body

- To begin the practice, stand with your feet slightly wider than hip width. Even with this relatively wide stance, you should still be comfortable. Unlock the knees just enough to show a slight bend. Sink into the Earth through your Bubbling Spring points. Relax the pelvis, lower back, and abdomen. Feel the connection to the universe from the crown of your head, through the Bai Hui point. This connection lifts the spine and allows a relaxed erectness of the whole body. Your arms are relaxed and fall straight down from comfortable shoulders. Feel yourself deeply connected to Gaia through your feet. Close your eyes and breathe from the belly.

- Begin the movement by very gently lifting your arms. As the arms rise alongside the body, the palms face up. Be sure the shoulders and elbows remain relaxed. Let your arms continue floating upward until they form a semicircle above the crown of the head. Pause when your fingertips are about six to twelve inches apart from each other. Establish an energetic connection between the Laogong points in the center of your palms and the Bai Hui point at the crown of your head.

- Then very softly, very slowly, and very gently, swing your hands down over the forehead with your palms facing down. Bring your hands down the front centerline of your body and feel the qi. The qi moves down into the marrow of the skull, and it continues washing down through the marrow of all your bones, from the skull to

The bone marrow washing exercise

the foot bones, as your hands continue to fall. The arms rotate naturally as they slowly drop. The fingertips should be facing one another, two to four inches apart, and your palms continue to face down. The hands maintain their descent along the centerline of the body, always staying about two to six inches away from the torso, and never touching the body. They drop down past the third eye area, the nose, the mouth, the throat, the chest and thymus, and then the middle part of the torso, on down past the lower abdomen and genitals. When your hands reach the genital area, they separate and the palms turn up as the arms rise out and up again in preparation for the next pass.

Coordinating Your Breath with Your Mind

- During your very slow first exhalation, coordinate the movement of your hands with the intention of your mind. Gradually lower your hands as you move your mind through the marrow of all of your bones for the duration of your out-breath. If you cannot do it all in one breath, then just breathe naturally while you focus on the cleansing action of the qi pouring throughout the bone marrow as you exhale. The primary aim is to feel the qi entering the crown of the head and moving down through the entire skeletal structure. All obscurations, impurities, toxins, and blockages are completely cleansed and purified. This process removes any stuck or stagnant energy in your bone marrow.

Repeating the Flow—Concentrating on Specific Bone Structures

In summary, this stage purifies all the bones and the bone marrow in the body. On each repetition of the movement, various parts of the body are emphasized with an accompanying visualization. The visualization is of Heaven qi coming in from above as the arms lift up. As the palms move down, visualize the qi purifying and rejuvenating the bones, joints, and bone marrow. When the qi finally exits the body, visualize it as liquid light energy coming out through your feet. All the toxins and negativities are carried away and transmuted into a fertilizer for Gaia.

The practice is presented in greater detail further on, but for now, here is a brief example:

- First, as your hands lower from the crown of your head down to your skull, see in your mind's eye Heaven qi purifying the bone marrow of the skull as your hands move palm down in front of your head. Then envision the Heaven qi continuing down, purifying the vertebrae of the neck.

- The sequence continues through the bones, joints, and bone marrow of the following areas:

  - Shoulders and scapulae

  - Arms

  - Hands

  - Fingers

  - Rib cage (front and back), ribs, and sternum

  - Several passes over the entire backbone from your skull all the way down to the coccyx

  - Pelvic girdle (pelvis, coccyx, sacrum)

  - Thighs

  - Knees

- Lower legs

- Ankles

- Feet

- Toes

- When the hands complete their descent, visualize the Heaven qi flowing out from the K1 points and the soles of the feet as pure liquid light energy. See this energy carrying away all form of negativity, blockages, tensions, and toxins—leaving behind only fresh qi and revitalized bones.

Repeating the Flow—Invoking Additional Cosmic and Earth Energies

Begin another pass, even more detailed. This time, along with the Heaven qi coming down into your crown from above, you can also feel your crown absorbing many additional specific sources of universal energy. Identify and connect with as many of these specific cosmic and Earth-based energies as you feel comfortable with. By envisioning these energies in more detail, it allows much more specific forms of qi to be added to the marrow-washing practice.

Some of these additional sources of energy include the rainbow-colored energies coming in from our Solar System, the red light coming from the Big Dipper star system, the violet energy of the North Star, the golden force flowing in from our home Milky Way Galaxy, and from even more distant realms of the universe. All these energies join the Heaven qi flowing into the crown of your head.

If you wish, you can also feel all the pores in your body absorbing fresh qi from plants, stones, Mother Earth, the air, the Earth's waters, and the Sun's rays.

- Let your hands float up from your sides and float up above your head, and this time feel all the beautiful healing qi coming in through the crown of your head as you begin to move the hands down in front of your body, in front of your head, and in front of your torso. Maintain your hand position with your fingers pointing towards each other as the hands move down, very slowly, in a totally relaxed manner.

- Feel the healing qi enter into the crown of the head. This time it purifies the bone marrow of the skull, all of the structures of the skull, the bone marrow of the jaw, and the teeth. It moves on down into the neck and through the bone marrow of the neck, and then washes the bone marrow of the bones of the left and the right shoulders. This completes the first pass.

- Let the arms rise up again and begin a second pass. As the arms and hands lift, gather in the qi from all the sources. When the hands are above the crown of your head, your fingertips should be facing one another six to twelve inches apart. Establish an energetic connection between the Laogong points in the center of your palms with the Bai Hui point at the crown of your head. Feel the qi again ready to descend.

- This time, feel the qi moving down and washing the bones and the bone marrow of your upper arms, elbows, and forearms, then on down through the bones and bone marrow of your hands and fingers.

- Once again, your arms float up over the crown of your head and make another pass. You feel the qi moving through the scapula, through the rib cage of the front of the body, all the ribs, the sternum, the scapula of the back, the upper back, all the bones associated with the ribs and the back of the body, and the bone marrow of both the front and back of the rib cage. Focus upon gently purifying and cleansing the bone marrow as you move your hands down.

- Once more, allow your hands to float up. This time as your hands connect with the Bai Hui point, you are going to purify the bone marrow of the entire spine. Feel the qi moving down through the crown of the head and through the core bone structure of the skull, and washing the vertebrae where they meet the skull. As the hands move down, your out-breath and your intention guide the purifying qi into deep penetration of all the bones of the entire spinal structure. Very slowly and very powerfully, the energy travels from the upper vertebrae on down through the middle region of the back, and downward through the lower back. Finally, the purifying qi moves through the core of the coccyx itself.

- Your hands and arms float up yet again, above the Bai Hui point, above the crown. This time feel your hands move down in front of the body as the qi washes the entire pelvic girdle. Completely purify the pelvis. Once you feel the purification is complete, feel and visualize the qi moving down through the bone marrow of the thighbones. The marrow in these femur bones produces the majority of your new red blood cells, so send your appreciation and gratitude along with this purifying pass. As you complete this cycle, allow your arms to rest at your sides. Relax your entire body with some slow deep breaths into your belly. Be mindful not to force this practice. Relax and enjoy all the wonderful sensations.

- Now working with your lower legs, let the arms float out and up from the sides of the body. With clear intention, the palms sink down as you feel the flow of qi moving down through the knees, purifying the bone marrow of all the knee bones; on down through the lower legs, then penetrating into the lower legs; on down through the bones of the ankles; on out through the bones of the feet; and all the way through the bones of the toes.

- Again, your arms rise out and up for one last purifying cycle to wash and renew your entire skeletal structure. Your hands float up above the crown of the head. In one pass, do a final cleansing and purification of the bone marrow of your entire bone marrow system. This time move the arms down very slowly, reducing the rate of descent by half. They move down in front of your head as you feel the bones of the skull once more totally purified. Continue washing through the neck; downward into the left and right shoulders; then the entire rib cage; and finally out through the left and right arms, hands, and fingers. Bring your awareness to your spinal column and slowly move the qi down the spine from the neck to the pelvis. The purification continues into the thighbones, knees, lower legs, ankles, bones of the feet, and toes. You hands are now resting by your sides.

This sequence completes the first part of the practice. Your mind and your hands have helped to guide the flow of qi down from the crown of your head to your toes.

Cultivating Universal Energy Practice #6: Accumulating Qi in Your Bone Marrow

After completing the washing and cleansing of the bone marrow practice, you are now going to breathe qi into your bones from all the plants, animals, mountains, oceans, stars, the Sun, the Moon, and other beings of Nature. This practice can help you experience profound communion with the beautiful, fresh, open, and spacious natural environment surrounding you.

As with reciprocal breathing, be sure to ask permission to cultivate in this way and radiate appreciation and love to all aspects of Nature involved.

- Bring your feet slightly closer together so you are standing with your feet a hip width apart. Let your upper arms rest at your sides with your forearms angling slightly out in front of you with the palms facing down. The upper arms are naturally suspended and drop straight down from the shoulders. Your knees are unlocked and slightly bent and you feel your feet are deeply connected into Mother Earth. The crown of your head is lifting toward Heaven and feels connected to the sky.

- Feel the natural energies that all the beings of Nature would like to give you and share with you. These gifts from Nature will help you be a harmonious and integrated member of the whole community of life with whom we share this great planet.

- With each inflow of breath, visualize millions of tiny filaments of rainbow-colored strands of energy flowing in from all of Nature, penetrating into your bone marrow through the pores of your skin. With each outflow of breath, envision this energy consolidating and congealing into the core of the bone marrow.

- Breathe in universal qi andsense this beautiful, fresh, sweet energy filling all the bone marrow. There are literally millions of tiny filaments connected with different beings of Nature—with the trees, the plants, the animals, the stones and stone people, the mountains, the lakes, the streams, the ponds, the oceans, and all the vast bodies of the cosmos. You are totally connected by these rainbow light filaments to all the different beings of Nature and the cosmos; you are in communion with all your relations in Nature and the universe. Feel the combined qi unify into one great pouring of vital energy into the core of the bones of your skull. On the out-breath, experience the qi congealing, gathering, and completely integrating into the bones of your cranium. Then, intend storing the qi in the marrow. The bone marrow of the cranium becomes a storehouse of vital energy and regeneration. Repeat for a total of nine breaths.

- Breathe in and feel the vital energy naturally flowing into the bones of your neck and shoulders. Then, on your out-breath, experience this qi congealing, gathering, and integrating into all the bones of the neck and shoulders. Visualize storing the qi in the marrow for vitality and regeneration. Repeat for a total of nine breaths.

- Breathe into the bones of the arms, hands, and fingers with vital qi. On your out-breath, experience the qi concentrating into all the bones of the arms, hands, and fingers. Then feel the qi being stored in the marrow. Repeat for a total of nine breaths.

- Breathe in and direct the qi to the bones of your rib cage, ribs, and sternum. On your out-breath, concentrate and store the qi in the marrow of your entire rib cage and sternum. Repeat for a total of nine breaths.

- Breathe in that sweet qi from Mother Earth and Father Sky into the bones of the entire spinal column, from the neck all the way to the coccyx. Feel your bone marrow being completely regenerated. On the out-breath sense it concentrating and increasing its potency in the spine. Experience additional qi being stored there to aid you in the future. Repeat breathing energy into the spinal column for a total of nine breaths, inhaling and gathering this wonderful qi, exhaling and storing it in all the vertebrae.

- Complete this same process for the rest of the bone systems in the body: pelvic girdle, thighs, knees, lower legs, ankles, feet, and torso.

As you become more and more proficient with this practice, feel the energy from the Moon, the Sun, the planets and our whole Solar System, the stars, the Big Dipper and North Star, and the whole Milky Way Galaxy being breathed into you. Ultimately, you can invite the qi of the whole cosmos to join in.

Remember that it is your mind that mobilizes and moves the qi. Even if you cannot feel the energy, by simply moving your mind, the qi will follow. This happens whether you sense it or not, because the mind, breath, and qi are linked.

- To complete the practice; radiate love back to all the wonderful beings of Nature—all the beings of Mother Earth and beyond—into all of Creation. Be sure to include all the celestial aspects of Father Sky and the planets and stars, and the Sun and Moon.

- Feel your heart radiating back deep love and deep appreciation for all these gifts that you have received. Radiate love. Feel the sentiment and quality of love that helps to regenerate, heal, and repair any problems your relations are having anywhere in the cosmos. Send joy and blissful resolution for difficult circumstances that are afflicting any beings. Breathe out your regenerative love and appreciation. Breathe out this love from your heart for three to five minutes and relax into a feeling of profound love and appreciation for all of Nature, Great Spirit, and Creation. In these times of massive environmental abuse against Gaia, I recommend radiating some extra heartfelt love for Mother Earth.

- Continue until you feel complete interconnectedness and communion with all those beings who have shared with you in this profound energetic practice.

With this practice, realize that your heart has begun to open in a beautiful, natural radiance. As you move through your day, be aware of resting in this natural radiance of a beautifully open, caring, giving, and unconditionally loving heart. You are full, replete with a pervasive feeling of deep appreciation.

Opening the Heart

LOOKING TO THE HEART FOR WHAT IS true could be the most honest thing we do as human beings. How then do you access your heart?

When you first begin to connect with Nature, you are laying the groundwork for sacred union. As you explore the natural fusion of relaxation and presence, this exploration opens a spontaneous flow of universal life energy that surrounds you and pulses through you. When you surrender to this powerful flow of life force energy, you may experience it as openhearted joy—even bliss.

As you actively engage these essentialized wisdom teachings and principles for spiritual awakening in the wild, you begin to let go of analytical thoughts, worrisome emotions, and concerns about time. When universal energy permeates every cell of your body, a beautiful and amazing thing happens: Your heart naturally opens in a state of unconditional love. This blissful experience of unconditional love flows solely from trusting the union of relaxation, presence, and the flow of life force, qi. Cultivating qi through Qi Gong and shamanic practices dissolves blockages and generates the natural happiness of simply being alive and aware.

At the level of pure Being, all of life shares an unfettered state of joy and happiness. Trees, flowers, birds, and animals, all forms making up Gaia, are endlessly joined in a free-flowing dance of interweaving Creation. Once you open and surrender to this dance by gracefully merging in union with Gaia, you begin to see your own heart's joy mirrored in all forms of life. Liberate yourself from the need to label the things in Nature. Recognize that you and all other forms found within Gaia are constantly changing expressions of the Great Mystery beyond all fixed notions. Prepare yourself to encounter the wonder of the nameless and touch the vastness that holds the cosmos.

Nature is truthful, direct, loving, and fundamentally supportive—even in death. When you are in Nature, it is crucial to be in an open and receptive state. Start by consciously relaxing contractions, deepening into letting go, and trusting. Completely surrender into Nature, into the precise moment and place where you are. At a certain point you will begin to feel joyful and filled with a natural radiance. Trust the natural essence of your heart and surrender into that loving radiance. Your heart will open if you allow it. Let this state of unconditional love arise in a relaxed way—a gift of inner nature in union with outer nature. Rest in the natural radiance of the open heart. The ability to both actively and receptively open our heart is very important to our culture and to the world at this time.

It is a delight to be able to share the radiance of openhearted bliss and to realize that basic happiness is not dependent upon any particular contrived condition. Bliss is a spontaneous, open state that naturally arises. This arising occurs when you completely surrender into universal energy with an open heart. The experience of universal energy manifests in your awareness as extraordinary bliss. But bliss is not the end of the way. In subsequent chapters you will explore means to move beyond the state of bliss brought on by your open, radiant heart.

Opening the Central Channel

I would like to share an experience I had back in the 1970s, when I had been doing practices related to opening the heart and cultivating universal energy. Since the 1950s, I had been cultivating several Buddhist meditative and Qi Gong practices to store qi in my lower tantien. I practiced these awareness and energy meditations for many hours each day for decades. In addition, in the early 1970s, I began a deep immersion in T'ai Chi Ch'uan. Concurrently, I was initiated into Siddha Yoga with Swami Muktananda. During the same period of the 1970s, I was also spending much of each year with my Hindu teacher, Vasudev, in deep engagement in Hindu Tantric culture in North India and the Himalayas. My studies with him centered on opening a profound communion with the Divine feminine, particularly in the forms of Bagalama, Kali, and Durga.

After all these years and decades of multifaceted cultivation, I began to feel an odd sensation in my lower abdomen. At first, I thought I might have had the stomach flu or something of that sort. These painful feelings went on for a couple of weeks.

One morning, the feelings in my tantien transformed from pain into a sensation of something like warm liquid honey. This warm sensation began to bubble up internally. It felt like it was steaming up through the core of my body. This incredible steaming sensation continued, unceasingly rising up through the core of my body, lifting higher and higher internally over a period of about a week. Finally, it entered the crown of my head.

When it reached my head, I felt as if my entire crown had opened to the sky, and I went into a state of extraordinary, profound bliss. I experienced both my crown chakra and my heart release in a powerful way. It was so strong that I had no control over it. I went into a blissful state that lasted without a break for about nine months. In the process of this opening, I gradually relearned how to function with my rational mind again. It took some time because I was in such a state of ecstasy and bliss. Happily, that state is still accessible whenever my errant mind realizes its true nature and rests in primordial awareness.

Later on, I learned that this was a fairly classical experience of a powerful central channel or Kundalini opening. This type of event often leads to an intense opening of both the heart and crown chakras into unconditional love and pure awareness. What was surprising to me was how suddenly and spontaneously it happened when the moment was matured. Even though I had been doing some advanced meditative and yogic practices, I believe the real cause of my opening was basically uncomplicated. I was simply following the first three principles that we have already talked about—relaxation, presence, and cultivating universal energy. As such, their union in me was also my initiation into what has now become the twelve principles of natural liberation.

Many masters who have developed the capacity to open central channel or Kundalini shakti at will, are able to enter and remain in associated states of profound bliss for long periods of time. This kind of opening can happen quite unexpectedly on the path to deep spiritual growth. It is a wonderful sign. However, it is not a stage in which you want to solidify yourself. That could become a powerful attachment to bliss that actually blocks further spiritual unfolding. Nevertheless, if one can cut through any attachments to the ecstasy, such birthing of bliss is a tremendous blessing from Great Spirit, Mother Earth, and from the Source that births us all.

Whale Blessings

Whenever I think of resting in the radiance of the open heart, I always think back to an experience that I had in the 1980s at our

Sacred Passage camp in southern Baja California. I was there during the time that gray whales were migrating from the northern Pacific to Baja's breeding and calving grounds.

In the area where I live, the Pacific Ocean drops very steeply to the ocean floor. This area is also the southernmost extension of the Sonoran Desert, so the air is pristine and clear. Nearby is a desert mountain range that comes from the interior right to the coast. The area has a unique quality of mountains, desert, and ocean all merging together in one place. The humidity is so low that the air has incredible clarity. One can look out over the vastness of the ocean to see the subtle curving of the Earth's horizon.

One of the best things about this area is that the gray whales arrive and play in the sea close to the shore. Blue, sperm, humpback, and killer whales visit this area too. They all can come in close to shore because the land underwater drops abruptly into the depths of the ocean. This steepness of the undersea shore creates massive and powerful waves. As the waves hammer the coast, you can feel the reverberations up to a mile inland. Also, this area is quite extraordinary in that it still has extensive stretches of wild, undeveloped coast.

When people do Sacred Passage solos in Baja, they can sit in a cove for a week of solitude and have whales come right up to within fifty yards of them. They do not have to get in a boat and chase them around as most of the whale tours do. One simply enters a deep meditative state and the whales come. They sense when people are in profound communion.

I do not think that humans can really quite comprehend the consciousness of whales. Compared to people, they have huge brains; also, the segment of the brain we usually associate with high intelligence and communication is quite large in comparison to ours. They almost certainly have developed skills of perception and consciousness that we can only speculate about. From my many years in close proximity to the grays, I have a personal sense that their state of awareness encompasses a galactic level of being.

By contrast, human consciousness, even if somewhat evolved, is planetary at best, and normally is limited to one's own immediate ego, family, and human community. If my intuitions about this are correct, we have a great deal to learn from our cetacean sisters and brothers.

Along this coast about ten years ago, I had an amazing heart-opening experience. I was walking along the shores of these vast white beaches, empty of people, and I found a nice spot to sit near the beach's steep drop-off. I built myself a meditation seat in the sand and crossed my legs, facing directly out into the ocean. I positioned myself so that I was slightly above the highest of the wave break points. It was late in the afternoon. The orange sphere of the Sun was beginning to set into the sea. I still had an hour or two before sunset.

As I went into meditation, I began a simple meditation practice of placing the mind on the breath. After a short while, I found myself deepening into an experience of opening the heart that was completely spontaneous and effortless. I had no intention of creating a powerful experience, but I found myself almost exploded by bliss. It was one of the most powerful experiences of absolutely radiant ecstatic bliss I have ever had, equivalent to the opening of my central channel. I began to dissolve in ecstasy and joy. The delight became so intense that I finally, almost like a drunken man, opened my eyes a bit and looked out to sea.

As I looked up, I saw seven whales directly in front of me about fifty yards away. There were four adults and three young ones. They were resting perfectly still in the ocean, but all seven had their heads lifting straight up out of the water. All had their heads turned so that each whale had one eye turned toward me. They were hanging perfectly still, totally tranquil in the water, with the bottoms of their bodies sunk straight down into the sea, with the upper third above the water, just resting there.

I could literally see the waves of radiance coming from them, and I could, of course, feel myself receiving it internally as I went into this shared state of ecstasy and tremendous opening of the heart. With my eyes wide open, I just rested in that state of complete immersion and the union in the radiance of the open heart.

In truth, they were sharing something that was a great blessing, and it was one of the most powerful transmissions I have ever received. One of the only equivalent experiences I have had was when I was receiving teachings from my teacher Dilgo Khentse Rinpoche. With the seven whales, I felt the same unconditional opening of the heart, the same extraordinary bliss of pure, loving radiance that I felt with this great, liberated Tibetan master.

Plants, animals, and other beings of Nature can be extraordinary teachers for you, if you give them a chance. Do not fall into the trap of thinking you know what something is just because you have learned its name. Names mean nothing. Names get in the way of the truth. If you learn the name of a tree or a flower, you fall into the illusion that you think you know that thing. You know nothing. It is better to be honest about it. You are totally ignorant. It is better to go into Nature in a truthful state of complete ignorance and say, "I know nothing. I am totally ignorant," and be open and ready to receive. That is the best attitude to have.

Tonglen with Nature

There is another delightful story that I would love to share with you. This story also took place in Baja, California. One of my students, Tony, went out on a Sacred Passage solo at a coastal cove not far from where I had connected with the seven whales. While out on solo, he went walking down the beach and came upon a seal.

A lot of garbage washes into the ocean these days. Somehow the seal had its neck caught in the plastic ring of a plastic six-pack beer holder. It was being strangled by this plastic trash. It was still alive, but was in tremendous suffering and difficulty. Tony walked over to see if he could do something about it, but the seal shuffled off, whimpering with great pain and difficulty. It was crying as it slipped back into the ocean. Of course he felt tremendous compassion for it. He remembered the teachings I had given on Tonglen[6] during the Sacred Passage Awareness Training (you will find instruction for Tonglen in the practice section of this chapter).

For the next six days, during the remainder of his solo, he devoted himself to the Tonglen practice. He said that the main focus of his practice was to bring healing and resolution to this seal, and for all the other seals and beings that were suffering from all the pollution of the oceans. This was the primary element of his practice.

When the final day came for him to return to base camp, he packed up his tent and got ready to come in and meet the rest of us. He noticed a movement on the beach nearby. When he looked, he saw this same seal climbing up onto the beach. He could see marks around the neck where the plastic beer holder had been.

The seal walked up the beach and came very close, so he walked over to it. He was amazed because the seal was totally healed, and the plastic holder was completely gone. It was quite clear that it had come back just to say hello and to thank him for all of his prayers and Tonglen practice. He was incredibly moved. This encounter happened within ten or fifteen minutes of his departure. It was the perfect completion to his passage solo.

Tony carried that experience back with him. He carried that gift in his heart and then shared it with us in our little group at base camp. Now you receive the benefit of his story and his compassion. This is an example of how, if you really apply the Tonglen practice in your everyday life by doing a little bit each day, it can have profound healing effects in ways that you may never know. It will definitely have tremendous benefit to many beings. I would encourage you to keep this practice in your heart and cultivate it for the benefit all beings.

---

6. Tonglen: receiving the suffering of others on your in-breath and sending out happiness and relief from suffering to them with your out-breath.

Opening the Heart Practice #1: Appreciation Practice

A good way to cultivate active radiance of the open heart is through intentional appreciation. Find a place in Nature where you feel whole and centered. Enter this sacred space with the intention to experience all of life with reverence and gratitude. As you notice the numerous objects in your immediate surroundings, send each one gentle appreciation from your heart. If at first you feel awkward doing this, relax and find something that spontaneously inspires you. It may be a gorgeous flower in the shape of a perfect mandala or the searing cry of a magnificent raptor passing overhead. The beautiful sight of a flowing, swirling cloud may be just enough to touch your heart and open that natural reverence you hold for all of Nature.

You could begin by appreciating a tree. Thank the tree for being the tree that it is and for all the gifts it has given you. Let the tree know that you deeply appreciate everything it has done for you and your fellow humans. You can do this internally or you can say this out loud. It is up to you. My main recommendation is that you truly offer your appreciation from the heart. A simple prayer from the heart has far more power than the most intricate ceremony performed without true feeling. It is a great sentiment to do something like that for a being you might have traditionally thought was inert and not capable of hearing and feeling, much less responding.

When you go into the wild, I recommend that you let your heart tell you where to go, where to walk, where to sit, where to stand, where and even how to attune with your inner awareness and your surroundings. Trust your heart to be an excellent guide. Trust your heart to teach you. Trust the inner guidance your heart provides. Let go of anxieties. Let go of business concerns. Let go of all the mental chatter that drowns the subtle, yet clear, messages your open heart provides. When you trust and surrender to the wisdom of your heart at that level, the world shows up new for you. When you allow your heart to guide you in this way, the possibility opens for Nature to teach you things that no one else can teach you; no human being can tell you; no book, movie, or Internet website can convey. Nature and Great Spirit can inform the depths of your being through your open heart.

Wherever your perceptions land, allow your gratitude and loving appreciation to flow. Let the experience of sight, sound, taste, smell, and touch open into natural, loving communion with everything being perceived. Over time with this practice, your experience of loving appreciation can deepen into one of union with all that is perceived. Instead of viewing plants, stones, or a brook as separate from you, let each sense bring you into the experience of union with whatever you are noticing.

For example, if a flower lifts its head in front of you, feel its petals brush softly against your hand, with no separation between feeling of the outer flower petal and the perception of the flower petal inside you. Experience the flower as one with you—one touch, one smell, one taste, and one view. Realize the continuum of that unique union with each perceptual field. Experience the touch of the petal as mysterious union, the unique union that *is* flower and you.

There is no separation, no division. You are simply resting in the perceptual oneness of sight, sound, touch, taste, and smell. This unified awareness affirms the communion of the open, radiant heart resting with inner and outer nature.

Walking with Appreciation

You can engage the appreciation practice as a wonderful walking meditation. As you walk in the forest, or wander among fields of wildflowers, or amble along a beautiful stream, notice everything that comes into contact with your senses. As you are observing your senses, consciously send love and appreciation to everything that arises in your perceptual field of awareness. If you find yourself walking by the banks of a stream, appreciate the flow of the water; be grateful for the rocks that sit by the side of the stream. As you are moving slowly and quietly through the forest, welcome the way in which the leaves shift and curl in the wind, or the manner in which the sunlight plays across their surfaces.

Appreciate the beauty of the trees adorning the banks of the stream. Be thankful for everything that comes within the field of your experience and through each of your senses as you walk through Nature. If you notice any small animals or birds, simply extend your appreciation to them for being there—for being part of your experience. Open your heart in thankfulness. Notice any authentic feelings of love that arise. If they do, consciously send that love from your heart.

In the beginning, if you do not feel a strong love, just simple appreciation and thankfulness is enough. The primary concern is to begin to develop the process. Make this way of relating to Nature a habit and develop a pattern of giving thanks and admiration back to Nature for everything that you have been given. In our culture, there is a tendency to assume that Nature is there only for humans to use. Many people see Nature and her resources as something there for the taking. So, by turning that attitude around and beginning to spend some time actually giving Nature your love and your appreciation, you begin to establish a new pattern. Your heart will open in fullness, balance, and wholeness. This opening produces a wonderful state of bliss.

Making the Most of Driving in Michigan

When I was at the University of Michigan as a young student in the late 1950s, I used to spend a lot of time in my '55 Chevy going back and forth between classes and my home—a little cabin on the shores of Whitmore Lake. Although not spectacular, it was a lovely drive, passing through farms and forests, and over cattail-lined streams. During the drive, I often focused on giving thanks and appreciation to everything that I experienced as I drove. It was a very simple thing, but I found that I started to look forward to the drive to and from school. In many ways, the drive became the high point of my day. I was doing a lot of formal meditation in those years, about four to seven hours a day, but that drive was a time when I could sit in the car and radiate my appreciation for all the beauty of the forests, the marshy streams, the natural lakes, the flowers, and the fields—everything that surrounded me in this attractive world of southern Michigan. By doing this practice, I formed a new relationship with my surroundings.

If this practice is done consecutively over a period of days, weeks, and even years, you will be transported to a whole new realm of understanding yourself and the land. It is like trying to describe the depth of an archetypal love affair. Ultimately, it does not matter where you are when you do the appreciation practice. You do not have to be walking in Nature; you can do it from any location, as long as you are connecting through one of your senses with Nature. Obviously, if you can get outside and walk in Nature, it is even more powerful, more direct, and more complete.

Opening the Heart Practice #2: Tonglen Practice

Another active method for cultivating the natural radiance of the heart is learning how to help other human beings who are in a state of suffering and who can use the helpfulness of your radiance. This practice provides a way for you to share the beautiful compassion that comes out of your loving heart, your loving-kindness.

Tonglen is also a wonderful way to give something back to Nature. We have received so much from Mother Earth—the plants and animals, the very air we breathe. We would not have the food we eat, the homes that shelter us, and the clothing we wear if it were not for the plant and animal world. So this is a way we can give something back for all the gifts we have received from Nature.

Tonglen is a Buddhist practice, designed to create and radiate active compassion. It is a core practice of the Dalai Lama, and also of Avalokitesvara (Kuan Yin), the Buddha of compassion. The word itself means "taking and sending." Tonglen offers us a powerful way to give back to our sorely battered Gaia. By extending Tonglen into as many different kinds of environments as we can, we send healing to all of Nature.

The instructions that follow are based on traditional Tibetan Tonglen practice. They have been expanded and adapted to reflect a particular emphasis on Nature and the wild. In eleventh-century Tibet, the nomadic practitioners of Tonglen lived in Nature all the

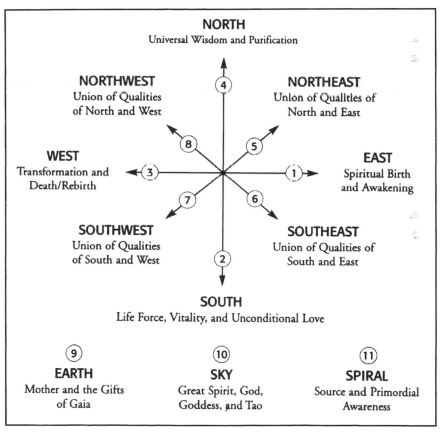

The Eleven Directions

time, year-round. Their practice naturally reflected this lifestyle. The meditation described here is designed to recall that easeful relationship with the natural world—a world that is too often far removed from our daily experience.

It is also important to point out that when you do Tonglen practice outdoors, your practice can be gifted with the fresh energies from Gaia; from Nature's elements; from the Sun, Moon, and planetary bodies; and from the universal qi of the star systems and galaxies. When these energies join your own inherent qi in doing Tonglen practice, one's compassionate activity can be greatly magnified and intensified. This leads to greater benefit for all sentient beings, which is the primary goal of Tonglen.

I realize that my suggesting the integration of energy cultivation into Tonglen represents a new dimension of Tonglen practice. Since it is new, I would recommend you begin applying it after you have mastered classical Tonglen. It would also be helpful for you to have worked with the Qi Gong practices in this book to gain more fluency in applying qi cultivation to meditation.

You can begin this amplified cultivation during the preparatory phase of Tonglen, when you are centering with the attention resting on the breath. At that time visualize all the natural and universal energies merging into you with each in-breath. Feel these energies coming in from Mother Earth; from Nature's elements and plants; from the Sun, Moon, and planetary bodies; and from the universal qi of the star systems and galaxies. Feel this qi being stored in your three tantiens, the five yin organs, the eight extraordinary meridians[7] and the bone marrow. Then set your intention that this is building qi for the later phase of sending out with the out-breath whatever brings healing, happiness, and liberation for the sentient beings you are working with.

---

7. The eight extraordinary meridians refer to the body's channel of energy.

- Begin your Tonglen practice with sitting meditation. If you are sitting Taoist style, in a chair, sit away from the back of the chair so that you support your own back. Place your legs pelvic width apart, with the calves dropping straight down, forming a ninety-degree angle. Tuck your chin slightly and relax your arms and shoulders. Place the hands upright on the thighs. Breathe from the lower abdomen—long, slow, smooth, even, and gentle breaths. With your head centered well over your shoulders and a general sense of uprightness and ease, feel your connection down into the Earth. Your eyes are open, but soft, looking down at a forty-five-degree angle.

- Relax. Let vital energy naturally gather in the three tantien centers of your body, particularly in the lower tantien. Gently rock back and forth and from side to side until you feel your spine aligned with gravity. Again, relax into the upright spine, now centered in its most comfortable, yet erect posture.

- Once your body feels centered, move your focus to the air moving in and out of your nostrils. Breathing in, gratefully acknowledge the gift of oxygen freely offered to you by the trees and grasses. On the out-breath, feel your breath dissolve out into all of Nature. See your out-breath returning your own gift of carbon dioxide as atmospheric food for all the plants. Experience your breathing as a direct, loving exchange with the wild.

- Now shift your focus to the clear pure awareness that underlies your breathing. Recognize the aspect of your being that simply witnesses everything—sensations, emotions, and thoughts. Rest in simple observation of all the forms arising and dissolving. Because it is without judgment or interpretation, this witness state is at the very heart of unconditional love. Pure witness and pure Source are unified. Recognizing this, breathe into the clear heart of yourself where unconditional love radiates. Connect with the radiance of your own loving-kindness in its most luminous form.

- Next, visualize that the atmosphere surrounding you is dark, heavy, and thick. On your in-breath, take this heaviness into your vast, spacious, pure heart. Take it in from every direction, through all your pores. When you breathe out, envisage that what you are sending out is light, fresh, and cool. Let this sense of freedom radiate from all your pores and disperse into endless space. Your in- and out-breaths should be approximately the same length. Feel for a while the texture of dark, hot, and heavy as you breathe in, and the texture of bright, fresh, and cool as you breathe out. Continue breathing this way until you feel the atmosphere has shifted, and that the bright, fresh, and cool texture has replaced the heavy, hot, and dark texture.

- Next, connect with an aspect of yourself that you find in pain or contraction. It may be pain over a past hurt, or anxious anticipation of something in the future, or anger that refuses to be quenched, or a painful longing for something you cannot have. Whatever form this suffering takes, touch into it softly. Connect with it as fully as you can. Feel its hot, heavy texture. Begin to breathe it into your unconditionally loving heart. Then breathe out whatever is needed to relieve the suffering of your contracted aspect. Envision the suffering dissolve as you send your happiness and positive energy to it.

- Next, connect with the pain and anguish of someone you feel close to, perhaps someone dealing with a similar contraction or form of suffering. Breathe in their pain and anguish and breathe out to them precisely what you can give them that will heal and transform their misery. As a caring person, feel into their pain and suffering as you breathe it in. Find that tender place inside you that is soft and vulnerable, and feel from there. Your heart unconditionally opens, taking in more and more suffering with growing compassion. Because true compassion is willing to take on the torment we typically tend to armor against or reject, the expanding compassionate heart becomes highly spacious. As you grow into discovering the vastness of compassion's unconditional potential, you discover there is nowhere for the darkness and weight you are taking in to get stuck or accumulate. As you breathe in, it simply dissolves in the spaciousness of the unconditionally loving heart.

- Next, extend taking in your close one's suffering and giving out whatever you have that can bring them happiness. Extend your breathing in to include all those suffering from the same type of torment. Pay particular attention to include your enemies and those you have difficulties with. As before, breathe out to them from within that which brings them healing, happiness, and liberation.

- Once again, breathe in suffering; but this time, breathe in all forms of suffering afflicting those on Earth. Now sense more deeply into the compassion that naturally arises when your heart is open, as it is now. This is free energy, the quality of which is total happiness, bliss, and liberation. Breathe out that bliss and liberation. Let it go and give it away. Give away all your happiness, delight, enjoyment, bliss, and even enlightenment itself to all the suffering beings on Earth. Give it away with the profound wish that all these suffering beings be completely freed of torment by your gifts. Breathe in their suffering with the aspiration that they be fully free of it, and breathe out your own joy and liberation as your transformational gift to them.

• Although our suffering often feels private and exclusive, the fact is that we share it with countless others. Whatever suffering you are connecting with, millions of other beings are experiencing exactly the same pain at this very moment. Recognizing this commonality, extend your Tonglen practice to all the beings who are suffering just as you are. Breathe the pain in for all the beings of the planet. Breathe out to them the compassion and spaciousness continually arising in your open heart.

• Now, extend your giving and taking to all of Nature in the wild—the plants, animals, streams, oceans, rivers, mountains, and forests. Extend this compassion to those beings of Nature that are under duress. Sense the incomprehensible destruction that humans are inflicting on Nature's ecosystems. Feel into the suffering of all these species. Breathe its darkness into your compassionate, loving heart, where it dissolves in space. Breathe out to all of Nature your own radiant compassion, light, healing, transformation, bliss, and liberation.

• Now feel the heaviness and darkness of abuse, war, incarceration, poverty, disease, loneliness, and despair. Feel all the physical and emotional plagues experienced by humans and other beings the world over. Breathe it in through all your pores, into your absolutely pure, stainless, unconditionally loving heart. On the out-breath, radiate relief and ease through all your pores and meridians. Send it out to all forms and all beings on Earth. Feel all human beings and Gaia in a state of harmony, natural integration, and freedom.

- Now complete the practice by extending out to the entire cosmos. Feel out to wherever suffering and difficulty may exist, anywhere at all in space, and connect with it very tenderly. Feel the tendrils of compassion radiating like billions of small hands, sensitively touching wherever in the universe suffering exists.

- Breathe that pain into your compassionate heart and, finding there an endless wellspring of compassion and loving-kindness, breathe that out as brilliant, clear energy that brings healing, transformation, liberation, and bliss. Continue this giving and taking practice until you feel completely and fully resolved.

- When you intuitively feel your practice is complete, very gently bring your consciousness back to resting in the clear, formless awareness. In this undisturbed, spacious state, witness the resolution of all suffering. Allow breath to flow in and out of your nostrils. Delight in the sensation of oxygen flowing into you from the trees. Enjoy your gift of carbon dioxide flowing back out into all of Nature. Completely feel that your gift, along with your love and appreciation, is being fully received.

- Rest in simple, uncontrived awareness until you feel complete. Then shift the energy back into the natural lower energy center of your body. Feel the steadiness of the lower tantien and your connection with Mother Earth. Sense your being as connecting the energies of sky above and Earth below. As you gently bring yourself out of this practice, feel the place in your heart where you can carry this wonderfully compassionate relationship with all of life into the rest of your day. Allow the radiance of your heart to continue gently touching everything and everyone as you go about your ordinary activities.

If you do this practice in Nature every day for twenty to thirty minutes, it will help your heart to open in a deep, enduring way. Gradually, you will develop greater skill in effortlessly bringing this radiant heart back home when you return.

Opening the Heart Practice #3: The Eleven Directions Ceremony

The eleven directions ceremony is a very powerful way to connect with the universal qualities contained in all form, with inner truth, and with the essence of the sacred view. The ceremony will help to deeply cultivate two qualities: your relationship and openhearted connection with all other beings, and clear recognition of your own fundamental nature.

This sacrament will help you establish a powerful relationship with your entire family of Nature. As you open your heart and express loving appreciation, your prayers and offerings will bring you closer to Nature in ways that will surprise you. Animals, for example, might begin approaching you without fear. When animals and birds become familiar with you and are willing to share their presence with you, they often become your teachers.

The ceremonial processes of great Earth-reverent cultures including Celtic, Native American, Taoist, and Tibetan inspired the eleven directions ceremony. The specific ceremony itself arose from the grace of Spirit's inspiration, passed along directly to me during my vision quests and Sacred Passages. It is specifically designed so that you can make it your own ceremony, which is especially important for many of us in the West who typically have little experience with Nature-connected ceremonial processes or prayer.

Modern people often feel awkward when doing ceremony that honors Mother Earth and the Great Spirit that flows through all forms. Or we may be doing a ceremony from a tradition or a lineage in which our culture has no foundation or background. Many of us do not feel quite right adopting these practices. We do not feel that we can really own the ceremony, because we cannot completely surrender to some other culture's sacred process.

For these reasons, the most important aspects of ceremony are that it comes from your heart, that it expresses the truth of your heart's natural radiance, and that it comes from the depths of your being. I recommend that you give yourself to this sacred process wholeheartedly. Incorporate it completely. Then the eleven directions ceremony will give itself to you.

Accordingly, the instructions that follow are offered as a foundation for the truthful unfolding of your own deeply personal ceremony. They are not designed to be rigidly observed.

Preparing for the Ceremony

Gather a few offering substances. Sweetgrass, corn, corn pollen, sage, tobacco, juniper, and cedar are all traditional Native American offerings. Copal is a wonderful aromatic smoke offering used in Middle America. In Asia, rice, fruit, candle flame, torma figures made of dough, consecrated water, fire, mandalas, and incense are commonly used. Tantrika include meat and liquor in their offerings. Or, to give the offering some special meaning, you might simply give something you like, such as chocolate or a movement like Qi Gong. Depending on where you live, it is always good to find out what has been traditionally used in your area and

155

incorporate that as an offering in your ceremonial process. Local beings of Nature and indigenous spirits appreciate that. Remember, the most important offering of all is a loving, appreciative heart. In making the offerings, envision that they are magnified millions of times as their essence is converted into delightful ambrosia that satisfies, liberates, and brings happiness to all beings.

As you move to face each of the eleven directions, always turn clockwise. See the directions as points on a sacred medicine wheel, or as complementary and interdependent parts of an exquisite mandala.

Performing the Ceremony

As with all the practices, go into a place in Nature where you feel inspired. Find a place where you feel that you want to give something back to Mother Earth—where you sense you can contribute something to the wild. This feeling of inspiration naturally opens the heart.

To begin, take a comfortable standing position. Eventually you can sit or stand as you become more familiar with this practice. Often the wind will respond to this ceremony and come in to join you, moving in synchrony with each of the directions. The joining of the wind is a wonderful blessing and confirmation from Spirit. Spirit speaks most clearly and directly through the voice of the wind, moving it in incredible ways. You can invite the wind to be your partner, your companion and ally for this ceremony.

You can hold your offering in front of your heart. You can place your offering on the Earth. I usually hold my offering up into the sky, and then release it into the sacred direction I am addressing. I hold the offering before my eyes, and I visualize its essence transformed into ambrosia with a potency intensified millions of times. This magnified substance becomes something that satisfies, brings happiness to, and liberates all beings as I make the offering. In this way, whatever your offering is—whether it's corn or cornmeal, sage, sweetgrass, cedar, tobacco, or rice—it can be a profoundly magnified offering. Its blessing can be greatly expanded so that it really brings wonderful gifts to all the beings associated with that direction.

Start by facing the east. Now place your offering to the east, the direction of spiritual birth and awakening. Again, you can either place the offering on the Earth, or you can gently toss or disperse your offering in the direction of the east. Pay close attention to anything that arises. Let whatever in Nature appears to the east—whether a tree, an eagle, or a boulder—represent the quality of that direction in that moment of time. This is how the east manifests in the natural mandala of your eleven directions. Do not try to apply a preconceived notion or artificial idea of what is associated with east to this sacred circle. Work exactly and truthfully with what Nature provides within the natural medicine wheel in that moment of offering.

Facing the east, make your offering to all the beings associated with spiritual opening, illumination, and liberation. You can thank the extraordinary guides and spiritual beings that help you with their teachings and insights in this way. Also offer your love and appreciation to all the plants and animals and other beings of Nature associated with the qualities of the easterly direction.

Now, turn clockwise to the south. This direction is normally associated with the open heart and the life force, the vitality that arises when the heart opens. In the Northern Hemisphere, the Sun rises particularly powerfully in the south. This is one of the reasons we, and the entire plant kingdom, feel its tremendous vitality in this direction. The radiance of the Sun also represents the radiance of the unconditionally loving, open heart. Make your offering to the south. Give heartfelt thanks and love to all the beings that are helping you to master the opening of your heart. Experience the power of your own qi and the natural radiance of your liberated heart.

Turn clockwise toward the west, the third direction. This is where the Sun sets, where all the forms of the world metaphorically die, dissolve, or are transformed. West is where we honor death, which is the precursor to rebirth. Here, we allow inner transmutation to turn those parts of ourselves that are ready for change into new forms of manifestation. West is synonymous with metamorphosis. As you face this direction, recognize your opportunity to let go of any old baggage and ways of being that no longer serve you. Just as the Sun sets in the west and dies for that day, allow your old thought forms to naturally disappear and die into the night. When you make your offering, feel that it is being received by all the beings associated with the qualities of the west—with all the aspects of Nature, all the spirits, plants, animals, stones, and elements.

Turn once more and face north. Just as south represents the quality of unconditional love and life force, north holds the quality of universal wisdom. It also has a purifying aspect that derives from that power of wisdom. Make your offerings of thanks for the blessing of universal wisdom, and for all the gifts you have received from spiritual beings, and from all the other teachers and beings, plants, and Nature that associate or dwell in that direction's universal wisdom.

Next, as you address the diagonal directions—northeast, southeast, southwest, and northwest—visualize the qualities of the individual directions merging together. For example, the north's universal wisdom and the spiritual awakening of the east come together in the northeast. To the southeast, spiritual awakening of the east merges with the qualities of vitality and unconditional love of the south. In this way, you will begin to see the medicine wheel as a unified field where all of the four fundamental qualities merge. As you continue turning clockwise, you join the aspects of all directions in a single mandala.

The fifth direction, then, is northeast. Make your offering here to the unified aspects of universal wisdom and spiritual awakening, and all those beings associated with those traits. Experience universal wisdom giving rise to new levels of spiritual insight as the process of liberation deepens.

Turn past the east to arrive at the southeast. Feel the qualities of illumination and spiritual awakening merging with vitality and unconditional love. See spiritual awakening helping give rise to a liberated life force, and a freed life force giving rise to a compassionate and radiant heart. Give thanks to all the spirits and beings of Nature connected with these life-giving, heartfelt qualities.

When you arrive at the southwest, experience the qualities of vitality and unconditional love merging with the profound processes of death, transmutation, and transformation of the west. Make your offering to the spirits and beings of the southwest, giving thanks for the dance of life and death, for unconditional love, and for the unceasing transformation of all forms.

Turning to the northwest, make your offering to all the beings that represent the unified qualities of death, transmutation, transformation (west), and universal wisdom (north). Give thanks for how death and the transmutation of all forms give rise to great wisdom. As with all the previous directions, visualize the offerings vastly magnified and transformed into ambrosia for all the beings associated with the northwest direction.

Each time you turn to face a new diagonal direction, you cross over the line joining two of the primary directions. For example, as you turn from the northeast to the southeast, you pass over the line connecting east to west. As you become more familiar with the eleven directions ceremony, begin taking note of these crossings. Feel, as you pass over the lines joining east/west and north/south across the mandala, the qualities of those two directions. Crossing over the north/south line, experience the unification of universal wisdom and unconditional love; and as you pass over the east/west line, feel how transformation of all form and spiritual awakening meet in the unifying energy of their opposite positions.

Having made your offerings to the eight horizontal directions, turn past the northeast to face the easterly direction once again. It is from this position that you will experience the power of the three final directions—below, above, and the infinite Source Nature—out of which all the directions and their qualities arise.

Kneel down to make your ninth offering to Mother Earth. Feel your grateful, loving connection to Gaia and the vast, nurturing abundance she steadfastly offers all beings that live within and upon her. See the essence of your offering magnified millions of times.

Now stand and, still facing the easterly direction, look up and lift your offering into the sky. This is the tenth direction, which represents Great Spirit, God, Goddess, or the Tao. Give thanks to Great Spirit, in whatever form you envision it. Then make your offering to all the enlightened beings and master teachers, human and otherwise, that benefit us so greatly through their teachings and unconditional love. Next, include your human teachers, thanking them for their blessings and tremendous spiritual help. Wish your living teachers good health and long life, happiness and deep immersion in the liberated state. Toss your offering into the sky.

Finally, turn in a slowly expanding spiral, feeling the entire mandala of the sacred circle being transformed into the sphere of Great Nature and Source. Feel it as a unified field of luminosity, clarity, spaciousness, and pure primordial awareness.

As you turn, all the directions and their qualities dissolve into formless primordial awareness, along with all the outer forms of Nature—plants, animals, birds, planets, Sun, Moon, and galaxies. All the inner forms of the senses—inner vitality, emotions, thoughts, and concepts—dissolve as you turn. This is the eleventh direction of formless primordial awareness. Honor the fundamental essence of this pure Source that rests within the heart of all being, and out of which all form naturally arises and sponta-neously manifests, and back into which all form effortlessly dissolves. Remain in this state of spontaneous presence, clarity, luminosity, and spaciousness.

As you remain in this pure awareness of Source, gently notice all perceptions, emotions, and thoughts. Moment to moment, recognize these forms arising naturally from the pristine state of primordial awareness, manifesting in its vastness and dissolving back into its clear light. Realize that you and all the forms of inner and outer nature, all the beings of all the eleven directions, are profoundly connected in this formless Source awareness. Continue resting in this recognition for as long as you can.

In every way possible, make this practice your own. Introduce elements that have special meaning for you, and experiment with what feels most aligned with your own experience and integrity. The central theme is to generate and express profound appreciation and love through the whole ceremonial process. If you do that, all the rest will unfold very spontaneously. If you perform this ceremony in the wild, you will find it leads to an incredibly powerful opening of your heart and deep awareness of spiritual Source within all being.

Cutting Through to Clarity and Spaciousness

IN OUR LAST CHAPTER I DISCUSSED HOW you could go into an open-hearted, blissful state. I explained this is the natural consequence of the union of presence and relaxation. When presence and relaxation are deeply cultivated, natural life force and vitality are released in an augmented flow from that alchemical union. This amplified life force is experienced as natural, openhearted bliss.

A potential difficulty arises when you remain centered in the heart's bliss. At a subtle level, you can become somewhat addicted to the bliss, joy, and happiness. Very often students of mine say, "Well, aren't joy and bliss wonderful? Isn't that enough? Shouldn't we just stop there and enjoy and appreciate?" I usually say, "Yes, it is a wonderful sensation. Yes, definitely enjoy and appreciate this experience. Rest deeply in the joy and bliss and happiness of the opening of the heart . . . but don't stop there."

As you sink into that luxurious bliss, it is very important not to get stuck there. At this point in your spiritual cultivation, a sudden cutting-through event can open up the immense clarity and spaciousness of the true nature of your mind. This cutting-through experience can bring you to the very threshold of full liberation. A profound cutting-through event can lay open pure naked awareness, and open the realization of your true nature. At the very least, it can give you a glimpse of the ground of being, and in so doing, clarify your path to liberation. However, Great Spirit, a skillful and realized teacher, or Mother Nature herself, must provide that cutting through.

Let's take a deeper look at cutting through to clarity and spaciousness. If you are working with a human teacher who is well established in Source awareness, it is quite possible for that human teacher to help you cut through. When you are sitting in a steady and openhearted meditative state, in relaxed spiritual communion with your mentor, at just the right moment the meditation master may be able to issue a cutting-through sound that will help to clear away all your gross and subtle obscurations. This penetrating sound can obliterate your buried levels of inner confusion. Such an abrupt cutting-through event can sever your attachments to bliss, and help to open up a very clear, spacious, free awareness—at least for a few moments.

Great Spirit and Mother Nature can provide this cutting-through experience for you, if you commit to refining your perceptions. As you refine sight, sound, taste, smell, touch, and the sense of balance, through your cultivation of mind and qi, you will notice and appreciate all five senses at an exquisitely delicate level. This is particularly true if you have been able to devote yourself to practicing many of the meditations and Qi Gongs offered in previous chapters. During one of your cultivation sessions, something very sudden and unexpected could happen. For example, you might be sitting in a beautiful aspen grove and suddenly a red squirrel sounds off in your ears, right behind you, with no warning whatsoever. This has happened to me many times.

When something startling happens, there are two possible responses. One response is that you could react in deep contraction, jump up, and think, *Damn, that squirrel disrupted my nice meditation practice!* The other possibility is that the moment you hear the sound of the squirrel, you surrender completely into the event in clear-cut presence. Experienced this way, the squirrel's cry can cut through all those sticky attachments you have to the steadiness and bliss of your meditative state. You can allow the sound to impel you into pure naked awareness, just like a samurai sword slices through all obscurations, laying bare the essence.

In fact, that wonderful bliss can be a powerful obscuration, an attachment that impedes your spiritual progress on the path. A wonderful being from the wild, such as a red squirrel, can actually serve as your teacher and help your awakening. The shocking call of the squirrel can clarify mind and make room for more spaciousness and lucidity within. It can serve to deliver you to the threshold of Source itself.

To allow a surprising experience to help you in your practice, the most important aspect is to not contract against the startling episode. Contraction blocks your opportunity for breakthrough. Instead, when an unexpected incident occurs, be precisely present, totally relaxed, and deeply surrendered into the event itself. If you can accomplish that, clear inner space may dawn.

Refinement of Perception

The refinement of perception is another way of opening to clarity. For example, you might be sitting peacefully in a state of tranquility under some trees. Everything feels integrated, harmonious, in balance, and perfect. As joy begins to arise, you feel the divine touch of bliss. With the refinement of your perceptions, everything is sharp, precise, and centered in the here and now. Then, above you, a leaf separates from a tree, floats down softly through the air, and lands gently in front of you. The very sound and sight of that leaf softly, gently touching the Earth is enough for a complete awakening.

An experience of complete awakening in the moment is called *satori* in the Zen tradition. In Zen, many small satoris ultimately culminate in one "great awakening." One of the pre-cultivations for awakening is the refinement of your perceptions. This enhancement is honed through regular meditation practice in Nature. Internally, you refine sight, sound, taste, smell, and touch to become extraordinarily sensitive to the present moment. Simultaneously, you relax. In this precise presence, distinctions between inner and outer nature begin to dissolve. A continuously deepening realization of the mystery of time and form around you occurs. The mystery that is you merges with the mystery of each form perceived. Suddenly the field of perception is severed by sudden, subtle, unanticipated change. Precise nowness arises and is recognized in the moment as the only moment that has ever been.

Recognize and utilize the opportunities Nature gives you for satori, a wonderful cutting through. Each cut cleaves closer to your true self.

To help inspire you about the principle of cutting through to spaciousness and clarity, I would like to share three stories with you that hold tremendous meaning in my own life.

Under the Arizona Sky

A few years back, I was standing in the Chiricahua Mountains of Southeast Arizona with two good friends, one a Native American shaman, the other a master overtoner. For many years I have led Sacred Passages and vision quests in these sacred mountains. I had just completed guiding a special vision quest for my shaman friend and we were finishing a Native American ceremony to give thanks for the powerful quest. At the conclusion of the ceremony, feeling happiness and great joy, we all embraced in a magnificent hug. I gently let go from the hug and stepped back.

Suddenly, and without warning, a jet fighter flew, at near supersonic speeds, right over our heads and just above tree level. Just as my friends were finishing their hug, there was a punch of sound that penetrated powerfully down through us and into the Earth. It looked like those guys exploded with joy from the heart. With the impact, they both flew backwards about five or six feet with a big "Whoa!" We all sat together and shared our experience. Each felt as if a great teacher had come and cut through every obscuration that separated and blocked the deep connection between those two hearts. Their hearts completely merged in that punch of sound pulsing through their embrace. For an instant, it blew away every last obscuration and sense of separation they had from one another.

An event like this is a good example of how this grace can arrive, totally and unexpectedly. Grace is what this principle is all about. Grace can come from your human teacher or from Great Spirit or from Mother Earth. In this case, that jet arrived at a perfect moment. I often like to say, "Synchronicity is the language of Great Spirit."

Of course, the pilot did not intentionally disrupt our gathering. Most likely he was oblivious to our presence on any conscious level. Mother Earth and Great Spirit, through what we normally call "coincidence," were demonstrating that everything is interconnected. When you begin to experience the world as one great web of interconnected being, one great web of communion, then you realize that all the form aspects are arising together. In this case, they were working together to help achieve a certain kind of liberation of the heart. It was an impressive event. A sudden satori. I will never forget it.

Cutting Through by Thunderbolt

In the early 1980s, I was graced with another powerful experience of cutting through to the clarity, luminosity, and spaciousness of Source. I had been asked to dedicate a friend's sacred site in New York State, very close to where my father had introduced me to gliding when I was a child. It was also near where he died. My dad died in the early 1970s in a canoeing accident on the upper Delaware River. After the dedication, I returned that evening to the place where I was staying, reflecting about the powerful dedication ceremony. My thoughts brought me back to the memory of my father teaching me to fly without a motor, and then to his sudden accidental drowning death on the Delaware.

It was probably around eleven at night, perhaps as late as midnight. I had just barely gotten underneath the covers when suddenly, with absolutely no warning, a thunderbolt hit me.

I still do not know where the bolt came from, although the nearby bedroom window was open. I instantly died. My spirit left my body. The sound of the thunderbolt was as if the entire fabric of the universe was being ripped asunder. I felt myself transported into a dark, whirling vortex, like the largest tornado you could imagine. I did not see any other beings in that immense vortex. It seemed like a vortex having the diameter of the Earth, or even more vast. Its length stretched out limitlessly. It was truly immense.

In my spiritual body, I shot head first up into, and then down the core of the spinning funnel. The dark walls spun by at an incredible speed. Then I saw the end of the dark tunnel ahead, the opening orifice of the vortex, which was at first a tiny, distant light of amazing intensity for its size, like a star. Moments later, moving at high velocity, I was thrown through an opening that was radiating brilliant, clear, white light. Then I dissolved directly into the luminosity, clarity, and spaciousness of that clear light. My personal identity dissolved. All being, all forms, all potentials had this Source as their deepest essence. The loving presence was indescribable. I cannot really speak very much about what it is like to become one with that clear light, but I can say that after death we all have something wonderful to look forward to.

The Tibetan Buddhist tradition emphasizes that if you can recognize that clear light at the moment of death, there is the possibility of full liberation upon dying. In my case, time was gone; conventional space was gone; forms were gone; there was only unbelievable clarity, unbounded love, and light. The experience was one of awesome space beyond infinity, and an intense luminosity that I cannot describe. There is no greater initiation than this union with the clear light.

At a certain point, however, my individual beingness re-formed and it was clear there was more to be done with this life. I made the choice to come back. I returned feet first, shot reversing through the vast tunnel, down into my body.

When I came back down the spinning vortex feet first, I was still looking back up into the light that I was dropping out of. Returning into physical form felt like precipitating back into density, the density of being encased in a physical form. The funnel dissolved and I returned into form. Back in my body, as my physical eyes started to function again, I found myself gazing out through an open window—the same window that I assumed the thunderbolt came through. My vision had never left the light as I reversed down the funnel. I could still see that now distant light through the window, in the dawning sky. Suddenly, I realized that the light I was gazing into was Venus, the Morning Star.

I sat there for a long time. Slowly, the room began to take on a clearer shape, the profile of the open window sharpened, and my bodily form became denser. When I came back into my human body, it was no longer under the covers preparing for sleep. I was not at all burned by the thunderbolt, and was seated in a lotus meditation posture on top of the bed. I had been gone for approximately six hours; the first faint streaks of dawn were lighting the sky.

I have no explanations for this experience. It remains a living koan for me. Although the event is hard to fathom, I am just presenting it as it happened. I share this story as an example of how the thunderbolt cutting through aspect of Great Spirit can directly initiate you into the Great Mystery.

You do not have a more powerful encounter of cutting through to clarity, spaciousness, and fundamental Source than death. A few years after my initiatory experience, I discovered that in the Tibetan tradition, there are actual lightning shamans. The only way you can become a lightning shaman is to be struck by a thunderbolt, go through the death process, and then somehow be returned to your body. For me, perhaps because I tend to be a uniquely stubborn individual, I needed some very strong medicine. This primal awakening was provided by the grace of my teachers, the enlightened beings in spirit who continue to bless my path, Mother Earth, Great Spirit, and the cosmos. For whatever reason, however it came to be, I am deeply and profoundly grateful.

We live in a time when modern technology is making it possible for people to go into a hospital for an operation, and then die, and then be brought back to life. Many of those human beings are serving as wonderful teachers for the rest of us who would like to know more about what happens after death. Of course, you don't go through the final death experience to the complete fullness of all that happens after death, because you do return into your body. However, you definitely get tremendous exposure to what happens immediately upon death.

Since many more of us are having this near-death experience in modern times, the possibility of liberation in this lifetime is increased. As preparation for the moment of death, it is vital to cultivate the ability to recognize and remain in pure, formless awareness, without distractions or contractions. For good preparation for your dying, I recommend regular meditation practice, Tibetan dreaming practices, the various cultivations shared in this book, and ultimately those practices that center on the opening of pristine Source awareness.

Whether you go through a near-death experience or your full death, prior meditation practice will help. Instead just seeing them flying by you in a fleeting instant, you may recognize the complete luminosity, spaciousness, and clarity that appear. In that moment, formless Source awareness arises as the boundless ground of your true being. In the Tibetan tradition this is called recognition of the clear light of pure awareness. If you are able to recognize that, rest in that, and remain in that; then there is the opportunity for complete liberation in that moment, in that instant.

The Natural Path to Liberation

Liberation in this lifetime leading to direct recognition of primordial awareness, is one of the main goals of spiritual practice. Any cutting-through experience, whether it's the powerful cutting through of the death experience or the swordlike event provided by your human teacher, or a hummingbird whirring suddenly to within inches of your eyes, or a red squirrel sounding off in your ear—any of these can open the clear space of pristine awareness. However it may happen, the grace of the cutting-through experience provides wonderful preparation for the moment of death.

Nature can abundantly provide this kind of grace. For the most part, Nature's grace will arrive in very gentle, subtle ways. This is especially true the more you refine your perceptions, senses, emotions, and thoughts. When your thoughts have almost completely stopped, a very subtle grace can come through and stop the world or halt the mind, opening you to the ground of being. Nature can be a tremendous help—a tremendous ally in this breakthrough.

A Tantric Gift from the Green Mojave

Another really powerful example of this cutting-through process happened a few years ago in Mexico's Baja California. I was teaching a group of students along the coast of southern Baja, and we had just finished meditating with the whales by the open Pacific. We had to walk back through the desert to get to The Way of Nature Fellowship Retreat Center in Todos Santos, where we were basing the Awareness Training. Walking back from the beach, the rest of the group moved out ahead of a student and me. The student I was walking with was interested in the systems of Indian Tantra. She knew that I've been fortunate enough to study all three of the main Tantric systems with some wonderful indigenous teachers.

Before I continue with the story, it may be helpful to share a little background. In America, Tantra is normally associated just with sexuality. Actually, Tantra is a vast system of teachings that cover many areas of spiritual development, including a small part devoted to sacred sexuality. The sexual emphasis involves integrating one's sexuality, and the power of sexual energy, as a potent assist to the path to full liberation. The vast majority of the Tantras, however, focus on other powerful and profound means of spiritual transformation. In all these Tantras, their power to transform one quickly is emphasized. This is why great care needs to be exercised in the teaching and practice of Tantra. If a usual but committed spiritual path can be described as a vigorous walk through both beautiful and difficult mountains, the Tantric way could be portrayed as blasting off in a rocket ship, where even the slightest miscalculation can have devastating consequences. And yet, if correctly pursued, enlightenment can be realized in a single lifetime. The three better-known Tantric systems are found in Buddhism, Hinduism, and Bon. Tantra itself can be thought of like a web or a weaving in which all form and phenomena are interconnected and threadlike through that web. In fact, I often describe

Tantra as the threadlike continuum of being interconnecting all the forms of the cosmos.

While I was studying in Nepal and India, my Hindu Tantric teacher, Vasudev, had said something remarkable to me one of the last times I was able to spend with him before he died. He said, "You know, to accomplish the higher levels of the Tantric system, you need to take once in your life, a deadly poison, like cobra poison, and transmute it spiritually without any medical help."

In India, one of the most potent toxins is cobra venom. The cobra has many associations with Tantra and opening of the Kundalini shakti, universal energy associated with the Divine feminine. Shiva, for example, is usually shown holding a cobra draped over his body, and often rising up behind or alongside his head. In Tantric Nepal, the Buddha, after his enlightenment, is sometimes depicted with a many-headed cobra—the cobra's body rising up along his spine and the hood spreading out above and behind his head. All this speaks to Tantra's power to energetically transmute all negativity. It also is a potent testimony to the path of universal energy as a way to full enlightenment.

When I speak of Tantra's power to transmute any detrimental form, I mean that the poison itself is transformed within the space of pure, formless consciousness and universal energy. The threshold this requires is a profound surrender and trust in the embrace of the sacred. Hindu Tantra necessitates a process of complete and total surrender to the Divine Mother. Particularly in her formless aspect as pure universal energy, the Divine Mother transmutes the poison into fundamentally free energy. Shiva, as untainted, unbroken consciousness, provides the companion field of formless awareness. All forms of negativity also dissolve in Shiva's vast, formless awareness. Joined together in union, the power of Shiva and Shakti to transmute is incredible. However, the surrender into pristine awareness and universal energy has to be one hundred percent. When dealing with cobra venom, if there is even one iota of holding back, you could well be dead. So, when Vasudev mentioned the test of the cobra, I thought I would put off that little bit of training for another time—maybe another lifetime.

I thought I had avoided that initiation until my woman student turned to me in the desert and said, "John, what is Tantra?" In the very next instant, I felt the fang of a rattlesnake enter my leg. It struck on top of the Achilles tendon of my right foot. What I found interesting was that I was pierced by only one fang. Many of the Tantric deities have one eye, one front tooth, or one breast. So, it was a non-dual Tantric bite.

As the fang went in, I could feel its potent sting. I didn't want to frighten my student, so I said, "You know, we really should head on back. I'll try to answer your question about Tantra a little later." I didn't tell her I had been bitten.

I knew it would be a good idea not to walk too hastily—I did not want to pump venom through my body too quickly. When I got back to the palapa, I let all my students know that a rattlesnake had bitten me. Intriguingly, this type of rattlesnake has very potent venom that is a neurotoxin, very much like that of the cobra; it's a relative of the green Mojave rattlesnake that lives in some of the Arizonan and Californian deserts.

There is a small hospital in Todos Santos. I could have been taken there in a matter of minutes and given antivenom to neutralize the bite. However, in the moment I was bitten, a vision of my Tantric teacher came to me, and I knew immediately, *Oh! Oh, I guess this is it.* It was a clear vision—he was resting in the sky right in front of me, looking at me with a bit of a smile on his face, and I knew what I had to do. I really didn't have any choice. I did not to go to the hospital.

Now, I am definitely not suggesting that if a rattlesnake bites you that you should not go to a doctor and get immediate medical assistance. Perhaps you receive the blessing, in a sense, simply by reading the story of this experience, and that is all that's necessary. If you are bitten, go to a doctor!

Initially, I went into a very powerful non-dual state. In some traditions this state is described as an opening of the third eye where you see and experience everything as totally connected, all forms as one unified Being. You and everything else are totally connected, not as an idea or a concept, but as an actual reality. You experience all forms as absolutely continuous with yourself, and you are absolutely continuous in every aspect of your being with everything else. There is an interpenetration of everything. The Tantric view dawns clearly. Fundamental Source awareness arises unmistakably. For me, this very pure state of awareness and interconnectedness of form lasted for several weeks. Of course, I was paralyzed at the same time, as the rattlesnake venom had worked its way up my leg and paralyzed it. I did get a little worried when the paralysis started to move up my torso.

If the paralysis had reached either the lungs or the heart, I probably would have died. But my Tantric choice had been made. Surrendering into this incredible awakening was so powerful that I let myself go into it completely, and allowed the experience of the paralysis to just be part of it. It was nothing special.

Once Vasudev had mentioned the need to transmute deadly poison, I had always wondered why one would go through this experience. Would it be to have a taste of the primordial, awakened, liberated state? Was that what it was all about? Well, it was more than that.

The next thing that began to happen was that many of my inner blockages—all those things that were in my being and were blocking the natural emergence of the liberated state—began to arise as my inner demons. Anger, hatred, worry, fear, greed, grief, sadness, jealousy, anxiousness, anxiety—every negative emotion you can think of—arose in me at one time or another during this experience. When these emotions arose, they completely possessed me.

From this state of pure nirvana, of pure immersion in the sacred view, my demons arose. All my blockages that prevented long-term resting in Source were pushed to the surface by the powerful energy of the rattlesnake bite. They had to arise, because I had not really fully earned the right to remain in the liberated experience. I had been given it by Nature, by the enlightened beings working with me, and by the grace of my teacher, but I had not really earned it yet. The process of really earning awakened energy and awareness was to embrace each one of the demons that was still within me.

So, over the next five months, I embraced every demon that you can conceive of. They were rising from within; I could not drive them off. The truth of my own blockages created their ability to possess me. Nothing worked except engaging each demonic emotion with complete and total relaxation, precise nowness, and absolute trust and surrender. As I relaxed into the ferocious grip of each demon, I carried it with me into absolutely primordial, form-less Source, into the essence of the universal heart.

Again, these demons were not external demons that came to get me. They arose naturally from within. They were my own neg-ative emotions and blockages. These were my own very personal demons; they owned me and I owned them. For the five months that they possessed me, they soon forced me to discover the power of Tantra. Nothing else would work—no purification, no ritual, no ceremony, and no antidote. Only one thing worked; when a demon would arise, I would simply hold it close in the Tantric embrace of pure awareness and free energy. I noticed that each time I embraced a demon, if I embraced deep into its heart with my own heart essence, I would arrive at the same absolutely crystalline, clear Source of pure Being. It was the same Source that allowed both the demon to manifest and my own being. At the level of pure common essence, I found the point of pure union. It was at this common point of deep, clear awareness that the demon would dis-solve into formless free energy.

After each demonic emotional blockage was transmuted in this way, I had a period of bliss and ecstasy—maybe for an hour or two, often as much as six or seven hours. At that point, I could finally get some sleep. Then, as soon as that period of rest was over, the inner energy would push the next blockage to the surface and the next demon would arise.

This process, literally, went on for months. I earned a new name among the locals of Todos Santos—Don Juan Cascabel. Finally, the parade of demons arising and being transmuted slowed down. Increasingly, I found myself in an incredibly clear state—nothing special, simply clear and light.

After five months the paralysis in my leg gradually went away so that I could walk again. For a long period of time when I was transmuting the inner demons, I could not walk because my right foot remained paralyzed even after the right leg and the knee regained mobility. I could not do anything with my foot. I never realized that if your foot has no liftoff at all—you really cannot walk. It was quite a lesson in paralysis.

My ability to move and walk came back at the very end of the experience. Because I could not move around during this whole episode, I just had to be with it. Rattlesnake venom may seem to some of you a rather extreme form of cutting through to spaciousness and clarity, but what a wonderful gift. What grace!

When I came back to the United States after the paralysis was over, I met with several of my Native American friends, medicine men and women, and almost every one of them said, "John, this is such a blessing." I remember one of them said, "I've been waiting my whole life for that initiation. You are so fortunate."

Before this happened, I would definitely not have understood these comments; now, I understand. I emerged feeling so light and so free. It was clear that this process taught me about how to powerfully transform my emotions. It trained me in the ways of transformation, using the cutting-through, Tantric, and self-liberation aspects to release and liberate emotional demons. So it has been a great blessing to me personally and to many others whom I have been able to assist with their emotional demons. I thank my teacher and the grace of the rattlesnake for this gift.

You, too, can receive this same grace from Nature, but without the rattlesnake, cobra, or thunderbolt. You can receive it by refining your perceptions—refining sight, sound, taste, smell, touch, balance, energy, emotion, and thought. As you become more attuned to your perceptions in Nature, pay attention to sudden surprising events. Notice when the grace of Great Spirit or the grace of Mother Earth comes for you. These gifts could arrive in the form of that red squirrel's shrill call, or the leaf falling softly on the ground in front of you, or the sudden shriek of the jet in the sky, or in the crash of a wave, or something totally beyond anything we can speak of right now. Remember this teaching and the cutting-through principle. When the sword of awakening cuts through and the gap of pure awareness arises, and if you can completely relax and surrender, you have a possibility for profound awakening. Surrender to it.

If you have a good, qualified human teacher who is able to rest in pure Source awareness, and transmit from that truth, he or she may issue a powerful cutting-through sound. Often it is a sacred Sanskrit syllable. In the Zen tradition, there is the sudden slap of the stick across the shoulders. Both methods can wake you up, particularly if you are stuck in the sleep of ignorance. Both function to snap people into very precise presence and cut through dreaminess and blissful trancelike states.

Nature, as we have explored here, provides precisely these same kinds of opportunities. In one incredible moment, Great Spirit can move through Nature's body to help you awaken.

Cutting Through to Clarity Practice #1: Rainbow Light Meditation

The rainbow light meditation is a very complete visualization practice. It reflects elements from many different lineages and traditions. Like the eleven directions ceremony, it is a universal practice, not owned by any particular tradition or lineage, yet in harmony with all the great ones. I received the practice itself during several visionary experiences while in the wilderness on a Sacred Passage. This meditation honors and provides a very deep bond with Mother Earth. It is helpful in cutting through to spaciousness and clarity, in that it trains us to refine our perceptions through the visualization; this perceptual refinement prepares us to use sudden sensory experiences as opportunities to awaken and deepen awareness.

The Smiling Down Practice Phase

- Arrange your body in a very relaxed and comfortable posture, either seated in a chair or in a cross-legged meditation pose. Your back and spine should be fully erect and straight, but with a sense of ease. If you are sitting in a chair, make sure the angle at which your calves fall from your thighs is arranged at a ninety-degree right angle. Avoid leaning into the back of the chair—the natural erectness of your spine should be all that is supporting you. Feel into your connection to the Earth through your feet.

- Find a point of balance in your torso by first resting the mind in the lower tantien, and then gently swaying backward and forward. Rock your body ever so slightly from the pelvis until you find a point where the whole upper torso is in perfect equilibrium. Then rock side to side in the same way until you find the balance point; your body is being pulled neither forward nor backward, neither left nor right. To ensure that your torso is perfectly balanced, move in a tiny, clockwise spiral. When you find the right position, you will feel kind of a natural ease and warmth in the lower tantien. Just stay with that. You should be able to maintain this balanced position exerting minimal energy.

- Relax your shoulders and pull your chin in slightly so that your ears are aligned directly over your shoulders. Your hands can be gently folded, or else you can rest them on your thighs, palms either up or down. For visualization practice, it is best to close your eyes—but maintain an alert and present state, even with your eyes closed. Place your tongue gently on the roof of the upper palate or behind the upper front teeth. Breathe deeply from your belly—relaxed, soft, smooth, slow, fine, even, steady breaths. Scan your body for tension or anxiety, and let stress go wherever you discover it.

- Generate a warm, gentle inner smile and a relaxed outer smile. Feeling very comfortable and internally alert, bring this warm, friendly, loving feeling into your eyes and then let it flow through your whole body, starting with the crown and moving slowly down to the soles of your feet.

- Guide the smiling energy, with thorough awareness, down over the surface of your skin. Then repeat, moving deeper into the tissues and muscles. Continue by smiling lovingly into all the internal organs, the endocrine glands and other internal structures, the skeletal bones and joints, and finally into the bone marrow itself.

Visualizing the Rainbow Light Phase

Begin the rainbow light meditation by visualizing a brilliant light in the sky above you. This light radiates like billions of suns all put together. Its extraordinary brilliance fills all the universal realms with rays of clear white light and all the rainbow colors.

- See the light emanating from Great Spirit.

- See the light as one with the essence of God and Goddess.

- See the light as the enlightened essence of all fully liberated beings, particularly those with whom you have a close heart connection.

- See the light as the unified heart and wisdom of all the Buddhas, Taras, and Bodhisattvas made manifest.

- See the light being emanated by fully liberated beings such as Christ, the Virgin of Guadalupe, Quetzalcoatl, Krishna, Kali, Shiva, the Taoist Immortals, and Kuan Yin.

- See the light as the Source essence of all the great enlightened teachers who have ever existed—and of all those compassionate beings who have committed to serving the highest good for all that lives.

- See the light as the natural, radiant essence and pristine Source of your human spiritual teachers in this lifetime.

- See the light as being identical with your own fundamental Source and deepest true nature—the clear light within you and all other living beings.

- Experience this light radiating out and filling the sky, and entire universe, with amazing luminosity. Its powerfully compassionate quality fills all of space. Countless light filaments—with the qualities of both light rays and liquid drops or particles—manifest in all the rainbow colors, mixed with clear white light. Some of these rays, drops, and particles come down and touch the crown of your head.

- If you are doing this meditation with a circle of friends, experience the visualization simultaneously. If you are sitting alone in Nature, see all the beings in your immediate surroundings being touched by this light. Once you are grounded in doing this rainbow light visualization with a circle of friends and with immediate Nature, expand the circle to include all of Earth's living beings.

- Now the light pours down and touches the crowns of trees, animals, birds, plants, mountains, stones, rivers, streams, lakes, oceans, and all other beings. All of Nature's forms experience this meditation along with you. They are your partners, friends, close relations, and loved ones.

The Purification Phase
Visualize a liquid rainbow infused with brilliant, pure, white light. This cleansing light touches the crown of your head and the heads of all other beings simultaneously.

- The light totally purifies all forms of illness and disease.

- The light totally purifies all obscurations of perceptions, emotions, and thoughts.

182

- The light totally purifies all of our difficult circumstances, both past and present.

- The light totally purifies all of our karma—particularly attachments, aversions, and ignorance.

- The light totally purifies negativity in all its forms.

- The light moves over the surface and down through the crown of your head; it then washes through the surface of the skin, fascia, muscles, ligaments, and tendons. It pours over your forehead, face, eyes, nose, cheeks, lips, mouth, and gums; it moves down and through your chin, down the sides of your head, through your ears, down over the back of your head, and on down into the front and back of your neck. Again, as this is happening for you, it is also happening for all other beings on Earth.

- Visualize the luminous, brilliant, purifying light moving through your left shoulder, down your upper left arm, elbow, forearm, hand, and out through your palm and fingers. Repeat this visualization for your right shoulder, arm, etc.

- Now the light flows through the skin and muscles of your chest and abdomen, front and back, completely purifying as it moves down your upper and middle torso. Light pours down the sides of your body and into your lower back, pelvis, and hips. It washes over the soft skin, tissues, and muscles of your thighs, knees, calves, ankles, and heels, then through your arch and instep, and over the skin and muscles of your toes.

- Gently bring your awareness back to the crown of your head. The incredibly radiant white and rainbow light is in the sky above you, pouring down into your crown.

- As it begins its second, more internal, voyage through your body, the light moves into your organs, starting with the lungs and heart. Feel it cleansing the air and circulatory systems as you breathe in and out; feel it purifying your lungs and blood as it moves through your veins and arteries, all the way out to your extremities.

- Bring the light down through your throat, esophagus, stomach, spleen, pancreas, liver, gall bladder, kidneys, bladder, and large and small intestines. Finally, the brilliant, purifying light moves through your reproductive organs.

- See this entire process unfold in both yourself and all the beings of Nature.

- Bringing your awareness to your nervous system, see your brain fill with white and rainbow light. See this light flowing down your spine and radiating out through all the nerve fibers along the spinal column, gradually filling every nerve cell in your entire body.

- Now visualize the light moving into your endocrine system, filling the pineal gland in the center of your head, overflowing into the pituitary, and moving through the thalamus and hypothalamus within your brain. It continues to move down into the thyroid and parathyroid glands in your neck, and then into the thymus, just underneath the center of the sternum. Experience the luminous light moving down into the adrenal glands on top of your kidneys. Visualize it purifying your spleen and your ovaries or testes. Realize that this light moves through all the beings of Nature as it moves through you.

- See the white and rainbow light moving through and purifying your entire skeletal structure, this time particularly emphasizing the bone marrow. Move from your skull down through the bones, joints, and bone marrow of your neck, shoulders, arms, hands, upper spine, rib cage (front and back), and sternum; and then flow down the whole spine into your coccyx, pelvic girdle, sacrum, and leg and foot bones.

- Experience this light purifying your chakras, energy body, and all the qi meridians and channels of your physical being. See it moving from above your head to below your feet. Watch as it cleanses and purifies your crown chakra, third eye, throat chakra, heart/thymus chakra, spleen/solar plexus chakra, the tantien (just below the navel) and your root chakra. Visualize the light purifying all the qi meridians over the surface of your whole body, from head to toes. Now see this white and rainbow light purifying and cleansing the energy meridians and chakras of all beings that you see sharing this cultivation practice with you.

- As the light circulates, experience its purifying radiance dissolving blockages, clearing obscurations, and transmuting negative energies. Stale and stagnant life-force energy is also purified. All these negativities flow out as dark substances, solids, liquids, gases, and energies from your pores, urethra, anus, and the soles of your feet. Mother Earth receives these substances as gifts from you and all beings and transmutes them into fertilized soil.

The Heaven Empowerment and Regeneration Phase

Repeat the purification phase sequence outlined above, allowing the clear white and rainbow light to flow through your entire physical and energy body. However, in this second repetition of the visualization, let your visualization emphasize the empowerment and regeneration of your whole being. Take as much time as you need to feel the fullness of this phase at the physical, energetic, emotional, mental, and spiritual levels. As before, while you do this practice for yourself, envision all other beings on Mother Earth sharing this cultivation practice together.

The Purification and Healing Phase for Mother Earth

Once more, for a third time, the white and rainbow light pours down from Heaven, through you and all other beings, down into Mother Earth. As it travels, it heals all human abuses to Gaia. In the process, all beings on the surface of our planet join together to become conduits of Heaven's light. Allow the light to move into and through the Earth's surface—its oceans, lakes, rivers, continents, mountains, deserts, forests, and prairies. Then envision it flowing deeper into the soil, rocks, sand, mantle, and substrata. See it sink gradually down into the magma, ultimately flowing into the glowing, red-orange heart center of Mother Earth.

In your visualization, all beings on Gaia receive this heavenly light and pass it through to the energetically pulsing core of the Earth. The light is cleansing and healing to all human obscurations affecting the health of Gaia, such as war, illness, famine, pollution of water and air, toxic waste dumps, nuclear waste, acid rain, deforestation, and destruction of the habitats and ecosystems of your fellow living beings.

The Regeneration Phase for Mother Earth

After you feel the clearing and healing of Gaia is complete, again bathe all of Gaia with heavenly light, this time with an emphasis on Earth's rejuvenation and regeneration. Take your time in visualizing all the same stages as before.

Now the white and rainbow light, in communion with the unique qualities of Gaia, begins to expand from Earth's core back out to the surface. Its melding with Gaia's red-orange heart substance has transmuted the light to a brilliant gold. This golden light continues to radiate outward toward the Earth's surface, filling every stratum until all of Gaia is regenerated and rejuvenated.

The Mother Earth Empowerment Phase

Now this golden light wells up from the Earth and into your feet, within the Bubbling Spring points. At the same time, the light radiates up through the roots, feet, and contact points of all beings on Earth's surface. Allow yourself the physical, energetic, and spiritual experience of union with Gaia as you visualize this phase of the meditation. This loving Earth empowerment grounds and regenerates you and all beings sharing this cultivation practice with you.

- Envision Gaia's golden light flowing up through your entire body, empowering every part of you from feet to crown, from skin surface to core. Include, as before, viewing the golden light moving through all your organ systems, chakras, and energy meridians. See it slowly flowing—like liquid golden light—up both legs, through the pelvic area, up through the lower abdomen and back, into the upper chest and back, out through the shoulders, arms, hands, and fingers, and then flowing through the neck and head up to the crown. While you envision these flows, feel that Gaia is empowering and regenerating you with her potent qi.

- You experience a rebirth, energetically and in your soul. Your first birth was from your human mother; this time you are reborn from the womb of Gaia herself. You have fully received Gaia's transmission and empowerment. You are now a force for Gaia to heal the split between people and Nature.

- The spirit and energy of Mother Earth embrace you and all life forms within her golden light. This blessing of communion naturally generates feelings of tremendous love and appreciation within you.

The Communion of Heaven and Earth Phase

The golden light of Mother Earth flows through you and all beings, rising from your feet up to your crown, and then rises above, where it merges with the clear white and rainbow light in the heavens. This ecstatic union of sky and Earth causes a magnification of Heaven qi, so that the Heaven light now flows down even more strongly.

As it flows down through you and all beings into the Earth, it unites with the golden Earth energy that, in turn, is inspired and magnified. You and all beings experience the simultaneous exchange and fusion of the Tantric energies of Heaven and Earth. In this powerful communion, all individual energy fields become greatly magnified and interwoven.

The Transmutation of Mother Earth Phase

The continuous flowing exchange of Heaven and Earth energies through you, and all of Earth's beings, now expands horizontally. You see a multitude of many-colored threads of light emitting from all the cells of your body, extending out to touch all beings nearby. These lateral shimmering fibers grow out in brilliance and extend from you to all the other beings in Gaia. A radiance of trillions of light filaments now interconnects all beings. The light filaments are a matrix of rainbow colors, gold, and white. As this totally interwoven light matrix unfolds, it heals all remaining negativities and obscurations affecting humans and other life forms. Gaia is then completely regenerated and renewed.

The entire Earth begins to transform, transmute, and manifest as a light body itself. It becomes a golden rainbow sphere of powerfully radiant light. You have become one with Gaia, which has transmuted into a being of luminous light. This Earthly light being lifts into the sky as the indescribably brilliant light of Heaven descends to meet it. The two merge in profound union.

The Universal Liberation Phase

From this total fusion, a tremendous amplification occurs. All the rays of white, rainbow, and golden light expand even farther, filling all of space and all forms of the universe. These rays heal, renew, and liberate every form they touch, whether an individual sentient being, a planet, a star, or a galaxy.

The Perfect Completion Phase

The liberating rays of the one great light now radiating throughout space, touch all imaginable forms and beyond. The rays contact all forms, which then become luminous, liberated beings, just like Gaia, and are powerfully drawn toward the great central light of Source. Everything merges back into that pure light of Source awareness.

- Visualize the Source light condensing into a primordial atom. All the forms, energies, and matter of the universe are concentrated into this single primal atom. This solitary atom containing all form, all energy, all emotions, and all thoughts then bursts out into unbounded space. An amazing radiance fills the vastness of the cosmos; then, just as a rainbow dissolves into the sky, the radiance dissolves into the infinite spaciousness of the universe.

- Rest in this natural spaciousness and clarity, recognizing these qualities as none other than the clear light and space of formless Source awareness itself. Rest in this clear, pure, empty awareness. As perceptions and other forms begin to arise—sight, sound, taste, touch, smell, balance, energy, thought, and emotions—simply recognize them as the rising and dissolving of phenomena within primordial Source awareness. Remain in this state as long as possible.

When you are ready to move about, gently and quietly shift into activity—but continue to maintain recognition of Source awareness as the source of all sensation, perception, thought, and emotion. Realize Source awareness as the ultimate field within which all these forms manifest and dissolve, from moment to moment. Maintain this sacred view as you move through all the normal activities of your life.

Returning to Source

THUS FAR, THIS BOOK HAS PROVIDED PRINCIPLES and practices that can help guide you to experience Nature as your temple, church, teacher, guide, and companion in everything you do. You are now ready to experience Nature in a way that can deliver you to the inconceivable boundlessness of Source awareness—the very foundation of your being and of all of Nature. You will now explore this limitless mystery and enormous dimension of spiritual cultivation in the wild. Your consciousness may expand to embrace previously unknown terrain.

The final principle in this book is returning to Source. Returning to Source is an expression that refers to the ultimate spiritual realization. Buddhists call this state "awakening" or "enlightenment"; Christians speak of attaining Christhood or Christ Consciousness; Hindus describe it as becoming liberated, or being one with God and Goddess. Taoists refer to it as "attainment of the Tao," and to becoming "the Integral One." Dzogchen practitioners refer to "full realization" and "complete recognition." Although expressed differently in various traditions, returning to

Source essentially comes down to the same thing—a dissolving of ego, the illusion of a solid, separate self in the greater field that unites and supports Earth, the universe, and all the forms of the cosmos, inner and outer.

In truth, ultimate Nature is none other than pure primordial Source itself. Of course, Source is a challenging concept to explain. It is very much like trying to describe the elusive, ineffable Tao, "the Way," which cannot be spoken or explained.

Having said that, gift me with a smile and forgive me for endeavoring to convey a sense of what I mean by Source. Applying what you have learned with relaxation and presence, you will be able to better appreciate the teachings of form, form-lessness, and Source that follow.

Each of us returns to Source countless times each day. Whenever you perceive something in Nature or elsewhere, you experience that object in its immediate, uncontrived beingness, free of conceptual overlay. It simply is. A fraction of a second later, your intellectual interpretations and emotional responses are activated, turning whatever you perceive into "other," something that you are conditioned to relate to in a certain habitual way. There is an instant underlying the immediacy of perception and then the illusion of separation. There is a clear space between one arising thought and the next event. Some traditions may describe this moment as the gap between thoughts. In this space of pure empti-ness, naked Source is revealed. In speaking of this, I am always reminded of the wonderful Buddhist Heart Sutra, which declares all form as fundamentally formless. In many ways, that view exemplifies the magical dance we all have with Nature.

The heart sutra also says, "form is formlessness and formless-ness is no other than form." All this incredible display of form that dances around you in your immediate environment is continu-ously and constantly arising from the depths of formlessness. Thus we see formlessness is no other than form. Yet, ever-changing form is formless. What exists now is vanishing. What has just existed is now gone. Thus we see form is emptiness.

One companion irony is that you become aware of the truth of emptiness through the form of your perceptions. This is quite a paradox to ponder. The mystery inherent in the world of form arises from great primordial, absolutely clear, spacious awareness. This emptiness has no particular content or quality. Yet from this underlying emptiness, which we are calling "Source," arises the entire mystery of the world of form. From this sacred view (that everything arises from Source), one also observes that all forms dissolve back into Source. All form is in a state of continuous arising from original Source, manifesting in the field of Source, and then dissolving back into primordial Source. As you observe this interplay of form and formlessness, you begin to discover a more fundamental aspect of one's inner nature.

Many who engage in spiritual cultivation stop somewhere within the world of spiritual form, and can attain high levels of profound union with all other beings. It is a tremendous accomplishment to experience comprehensive unity with all plants, animals, trees, rocks, lakes, streams, and even with Mother Gaia herself. To experience a state of seamless communion with all other beings provides great joy and exquisite bliss. However, there are even deeper levels of ultimate truth. One may even taste that which is beyond all levels, categories, and descriptions.

Discovering absolute, pure Source is beyond any particular quality that one experiences when communing with form. It is akin to the clarity of a mirror. A mirror holds all forms and it reflects all forms. It is visually boundless spaciousness, which is perfectly empty. The flawless, crystal clear reflectivity of the mirror allows all forms to arise, manifest, and dissolve. Realizing this unblemished clarity and vast spaciousness underlying the very heart of inner and outer nature is the ultimate practice of the wild. It can bring us into a state of complete freedom, even perfect liberation.

If you find yourself feeling trapped in your current situation, then you are caught in the very opposite of the liberated state. You may find yourself falling into a cycle of attachment and aversion. When you find yourself stuck in such a pattern, you are most definitely ignoring the truth of your fundamental self—pure and clear awareness.

When one realizes formless awareness is absolutely indestructible, the freedom is beyond words. In this liberated state, one tastes the ultimate wildness of Nature—the formless Source. There is no vaster wilderness than this absolute, pristine, clear awareness resting in itself. The display of forms only enriches Source, a magical dance of utter creativity. This is the true nature that supports us all.

Outer nature points to this constantly—if you only listen to what is listening, if you only see who is seeing, if you only feel that which is feeling. Allowing Nature to become your true teacher, you discover the undiscoverable.

Embracing All Form

In many traditions there is an emphasis on denying the Earth, denying matter, denying this world of form. The reason these traditions reject form and matter is to move practitioners into appreciation for Spirit, soul, and even formless essence. Such lineages are also concerned that attachments and aversions concerning form are a major cause of obscuring deepest spiritual truth. The ties that bind us are the ties of attachment and aversion that keep us firmly bound to ignorance of our true nature. Therefore, they dismiss the earthly realms of form in favor of embracing the pure, formless essence of Great Spirit, of God, and of Goddess. It is possible to deny form by saying, "No, ultimate truth is not this or that." This practice of denial can lead you toward formless truth, but it is not necessarily the only way you can arrive at fundamental Source.

Another way to arrive at this understanding is to embrace the whole world of appearance and the world of form with a resounding *"Yes!"* Everything is experienced as a phenomenal arising—a display of primordial Nature which is the original formless mystery that underlies the dance of all form. Forms arise out of, manifest within, and dissolve back into the formless moment by moment. Form is no other than formlessness, formlessness no other than form.

With this view, one embraces all of Nature. Then the entire cosmos becomes a teacher that you honor. One simply deepens the recognition of clear Source sustaining all form, both inner and outer. There is no denial or denouncing anything in the world of Nature. Your thoughts, emotions, and perceptions all become your teachers. The only thing being asked of you is to surrender to that truth so beautifully articulated in the heart sutra. When one accomplishes that, the whole world of form and matter can carry you into the free and open wildness of Source awareness itself.

In ancient times, the Taoist master Lao Tzu offered the following recommendation for returning to Source:

> Empty yourself of everything. Let the mind rest at peace.
> Let 10,000 things rise and fall, while the self watches their
> return. They grow and flourish and then return to the
> Source. Returning to the Source is stillness, which is the
> way of Nature. The way of Nature is unchanging.

This is one of my favorite quotes from the *Tao Te Ching*. This amazing compendium of wisdom and insight from the Taoist tradition of China has several passages that speak precisely to this discussion of Source and form. I often sit and contemplate the essence of this quote to connect with primordial Source awareness, which in Chinese is the Tao.

Thousands of years after they were written, these words continue to resonate with truth. I recommend that you sit with this quote and let it carry you. Because everything originates in Source and inevitably returns to it, all forms are innately liberated in the natural process of arising and melting away. We ourselves are liberated only to the extent that we surrender ourselves to this process. In surrender, we continue in the flow of unbroken Tao, delighting in Nature's spontaneous appearances and resting in continuous recognition of Source.

Dreamtime Awakening

A powerful experience in the opening of Source came to me as a blessing from one of my main teachers, Dilgo Khentse Rinpoche. One evening while sleeping, I had a very powerful lucid dream—the kind of dream where you are wide awake and everything happens with crystal clarity. I had been doing a lot of Dzogchen practice in a mountain wilderness. I think that practice, along with profound devotion to my teacher, really helped to support the opening of this particular dream state.

My teacher, several other monks, and I were sitting together in a large, light-filled hall. There was a circle of monks around us, and I was sitting in front of Dilgo Khentse with two other monks who approached him and offered a blessing scarf. He took their rosary malas, blessed them by rolling them in his hands, and then handed them back. When it was my turn, I rose and then sat close directly in front of Dilgo Khentse. We looked deeply into each other's eyes. Suddenly, he reached out, gently held my head and neck, and quietly pulled me forward—still holding our gaze. We both leaned further forward, and the crowns of our heads touched. In that moment there was an incredible opening of absolutely luminous, crystal clear Source awareness that engulfed everything—a vast, spacious, clear awareness beyond anything that I had ever experienced. Out of that clear space arose the sound "Ahhhhhhh." My individuality merged into that sound and the spacious luminosity. The gift of that initiation into Source has remained ever since.

Nepalese Meditation Cave

Several years back, I was fortunate to take a dozen of my students on a month-long spiritual mountain retreat in the Himalayas, at around 18,000 feet of elevation. We did our Sacred Passage solos in an incredible location—atop a steep ridge between 28,146-foot Kanchenjunga on one side, 29,028-foot Mt. Everest, and 27,790-foot Makalu on the other side. I guided this group of students to a spot that I had never been to, but had wondered about for years when I was doing work helping create Langtang and Sagarmatha National Parks.

Our chosen ridge rose directly north from lowland Nepal, lifting toward Tibet between the world's highest mountain massifs. It took us about ten days of steady climbing just to get there. When we arrived at the alpine zone selected for our retreat, I let everybody choose his or her solo camp location. The group was scattered out along the high ridge, with steep drop-offs on either side. I went to the upper, northernmost end and found a small, strikingly beautiful azure lake where I set up camp.

During an exploration of the area, I discovered an absolutely perfect meditation cave that looked like it had not been used in years. It was a triangular-shaped meditation cave notched into the center of the ridge. The floor of the cave was covered with sweet-smelling herbs, exuding a wonderful aroma somewhat like sage. A rock platform came out from the floor and actually jutted out into the sky. Directly below, there was a drop-off of a thousand feet down to the camp where I had my tent. When I looked right, it dropped down seventeen thousand feet into a canyon, and beyond the canyon arose Mounts Everest and Makalu. Looking to the left I could see massive Kanchenjunga. Beyond my camp below me, the ridge dropped down thousands and thousands of feet into the plains of Nepal and India.

There was no question in my mind that this cave had been used for deep spiritual practice over a very long period of time.

The presence of all the great masters and of Great Nature in this cave seemed to support my practice in this spot. I meditated in the cave and found that within just a few days I was able to go into a deep state of pure Source, simply resting in Source awareness. As I was meditating directly out into the sky, wonderful manifestations of circular rainbows appeared in the sky before me. After longer days of cultivation, even parts of my own body appeared to be dissolving into rainbow-colored lights. I felt all these experiences of form dissolving into rays and light were the blessing of all my teachers and of the masters who had meditated here long before me.

Resting in Source Practice #1: "Who Am I?"

An exploration of form, formlessness, and returning to Source may seem challenging or difficult to understand. Therefore, the best way to foster understanding within oneself, and to ultimately embody this realization, is simply to do some practices.

An excellent beginning practice for exploring Source awareness comes out of the Hindu tradition. The great Hindu master Ramana Maharshi perfected a practice that is often called "Who Am I?" Sometimes this process is described as self-inquiry, which is a practice that explores the truth of who you are in your true nature. It begins elegantly by asking the simple question, "Who am I?"

You will be looking into yourself, into your unique truth— nobody else's truth. This is not a truth about what your family has told you, what your friends tell you, or what your lover tells you. It is not about any of the identities you have convinced yourself that you are. This is about finding what is truly you. What dwells within that is permanent and unchanging?

This question, "Who am I?" seeks permanent, indestructible truth. As you pursue the inquiry of who you are, any answer that does not have within it the quality of permanent, unchanging truth is dropped.

Ramana Maharshi developed this practice in Nature on a beautiful hillside in southern India. Nature allows you to drop your false identities, as more of the essential aspect of who you truly are emerges. Also, your cultural conditioning and urban orientation are stripped away more easily in Nature.

- Find a beautiful and tranquil spot in Nature—a place without outer distractions. Return to a centered and clear awareness within yourself and generate a mood of natural relaxation and good-heartedness. As you do this practice, you will be dropping many identities that you may have thought you were. Feel a sense of relief that you can let go of any need to hold on to a concrete or rigid identity. Feel a sense of freedom. You can finally drop unnecessary labels and unwanted identifications. Maintain a kind and gentle attitude about releasing this excess baggage.

- Begin by asking yourself, "Who *am* I, who am I at a very truthful and deep level?" Every time you ask yourself the question, "Who am I really at the deepest level?" discard or reject anything that is not absolutely, unchangingly true. Explore this for a few minutes or more in silence.

- Continue this inquiry by asking questions similar to those described below and answering truthfully along the lines indicated under each question.

- Am I my name?
  No, not really, that is a very temporary thing.

- Am I my family?

No, that is also a passing relationship.

- Am I what my friends have told me I am?
  I carry many identities with different friends. My same friend tells me different things about who I am at different times.

- Am I the clothes that I wear?
  Not likely. They are constantly changing.

- Am I the car that I drive?
  This is obviously a superficial assessment of who you are, revealing nothing more than your preferences.

- Am I the schools that I attended?
  Are you the teachers who taught you? Are you the classrooms you occupied for a few hours? Are you the books you read or the tests you took? Learning from schools comes and goes.

- Am I the training that I have received?
  Not really. Seminars and workshops are variable events. Facts come and go. What is relevant now may not be tomorrow.

- Am I my bank account?
  This is only a steady stream of checks and balances, constantly changing.

- Am I my financial portfolio?
  With the vagaries of fluctuating value, there is nothing permanent there.

- Am I my job?

Even though your profession may be something important to you, it is still not unchanging. What you do each day is different, even though it may appear to be the same. There is never quite the same piece of paper on the desk before you. The play of light on your desk is constantly shifting, and the clothes that you wear are never quite the same. The way you interact with your associates in the office is never identical.

- If I am not all that, can I say that I am this body?
  Your body is not a permanent thing. Your body is constantly changing. When you were conceived, you were just the union of two cells from your mother and father. Through birth, during the whole process of becoming an adolescent, and then later growing into midlife and aging into a senior citizen, finally arriving at death, there is not a single moment at which there is any kind of stable, permanent essence of yourself in your constantly changing body. The body that you are so identified with, that you believe is you, is simply a magical display that is constantly changing. It is never the same. It never has been the same, and never will be the same. It is not the same from one second to the next. Every cell in your body is constantly changing. So each cell, tissue, organ system, and every other part of your body is in a state of constant transformation. Even the circulation of blood flow is never the same from moment to moment. You are continually receiving and giving out elements from your body. There is no point at which you are the same. So, this body is also a passing phenomenon, a moving mystery. It has no permanent, substantial reality, only a changing reality.

- Am I my feelings? My emotions?

They are also constantly changing. Sometimes you are happy; sometimes you are down; sometimes things are going well with your friends and loved ones; and sometimes you are overtaken by feelings of anxiety, stress, and tension. Things are always changing with the emotions.

• How about my thoughts? Surely I am what I think?
There is no stability in your thoughts. They are even more transitory than the movement of clouds in the sky. There is not a single permanent thought within you. Every thought is constantly changing—it comes, it manifests, it goes. It appears out of a mystery, it manifests in a mystery, and it dissolves into a mystery.

As you explore the mystery of this continuously changing identity, you will see that every form aspect in the past, even all your experiences of the past, are not you in this moment. Those experiences are no longer there, they are no longer truth, and they are not you now. This experience is the same for the future. You are not your goals, ambitions, desires, or fears. All of these are passing thoughts.

When you really examine all the elements that you normally identify with yourself, whether externally or internally, there is nothing that is permanent. It is a little like the wind. As you listen to the wind blow through the trees, recognize that wind never circulates in quite the same way. It never plays through the leaves in quite the same way. The sound never reaches your ears in the same precise fashion.

All the things that you identify with as yourself are actually always changing. They are never quite the same. There is nothing permanent about them or yourself. Therefore, this concept of a permanent, "I am something" is not stable. If you identify with something in the world of form, you're going to find that it will change. It always does.

Truth in the Moment

What is true is what is arising in the now. The fundamental heart of this great mystery is something like the clarity of the sky, the spaciousness of the ocean, the perfect reflectivity of a mirror that allows all of these forms to arise and manifest, and then receives those forms back into itself.

What I would recommend is that you do this practice for as long as you feel comfortable. Initially, it can be for five or ten minutes a day in that very special, natural place. This is not about finding some conceptual answer. Even if you are identifying with the concept of yourself as a vast, free, clear, spacious being, then you are not in pure Source—you are simply identifying with the concept of that for a while.

You may find that at certain points there is a moment when everything stops. The thoughts, the perceptions, and the feelings simply cease. There is a little gap between the thoughts and the feelings. In this gap a seed of truth of who you really are may arise. If this should happen, simply rest in the pure essence of that realization for as long as it is there. Do not grasp after it or try to grab onto it. Over time, there will be periods when you can rest in Source in a very natural and uncontrived way.

I urge you to practice "Who Am I?" for your whole life. It comes to us directly from one of the greatest enlightened masters of our era, as his highest recommendation.

Resting in Source Practice #2: Turning the Light Around

You have been exploring how your perceptions of sight, sound, taste, smell, and touch put you in a state of continuous connection and communion with all of Nature. These same senses can, with the help of Nature, carry us back to Source awareness itself. In order to experience Source through your senses, it requires turning your perceptions completely around. Instead of losing yourself in the outer world of outer nature, it is possible that you can trace each one of your perceptual fields back to their origin. There is a wonderful practice from the Taoist tradition called "turning the light around" that allows you to actually experience the point at which all senses arise out of a primal Source state of emptiness within.

Earlier, you explored the way in which your perceptions can be cultivated—how they can be appreciated as a way of entering into deep connectedness and then union with all of magnificent Nature. With the turning the light around practice, you will start the exercise in a similar way, but instead of resting in the continuum of connectedness, you will follow your perceptions back to Source.

As a metaphor, the turning the light around practice is similar to using a flashlight, but instead of shining the light out in front you, you shine the light back into you—into your Source essence.

Turning Sight Around

Simply focus on a tree. Let your mind rest naturally in the experience of seeing that tree. Feel the natural connection with that tree you see before you, and connect with the feeling of the tree that is arising within. That tree is as equally within you as it is in front of you, because you perceive it from within. It may have an outer reality, but the experience of it is totally internal.

Instead of going outward with your vision to see that tree, go inward with your vision to follow the experience of seeing a tree. Work at seeing the tree deeper and deeper within, to the point of origination within yourself. In other words, you follow the experience of the light of that tree down as deep as you can go within yourself. This process carries you into that very pure, crystal clear Source awareness. It takes you right back into the most direct and simple pure point of cognition.

Realize that you have a natural communion with the tree, because it is experienced totally within. Then take that feeling a little further; realize that there is truly no other reality than the experience of that tree within you. Then follow that feeling even further back to where it is being experienced. Where are you experiencing it? Where is that experience of the tree arising within you? Eventually, you will find that the experience of seeing is held in your pure being.

The sight of the tree is something like a crystal clear mirror. The tree is coming deep into the vast reflective clarity of that mirror, your inner awareness. As you realize that, you also realize that all these other forms of Nature that you see with your peripheral sight can be followed back into the clarity of that inner mirrorlike awareness. The inner mirrorlike awareness holds the experience of the tree and all other things that you see in the environment around you. Experience all of that internally, at the deepest level, and with the clear mirror of awareness.

Turning Sound Around

Follow the same process as turning sight around, but this time use your sense of hearing. It may help you to close your eyes to focus on sound. Normally, when you hear the wind you say to yourself, *I hear the wind. It is over there in that tree.* However, this time follow the sound of the wind moving through the tree internally, following it back within your being. Follow the sound of the wind from moving in the trees, moving into your ears, moving into perceptual awareness itself, and then moving to that place where you begin to label it as wind within your mind. Now, follow the sound even deeper to a level that is beyond the labels. The labels *wind* and *tree* arise out of a much deeper level of consciousness, which is clear mirrorlike awareness itself.

Let whatever sound arises carry you back into that clear mirrorlike awareness at the very deepest level within you. Find where the hearing happens within. Realize that this clear mirrorlike awareness allows the hearing of the wind moving through the trees to arise, to manifest, and to dissolve back into Source. There is really no effort to this. It is simply turning the experience of sound back upon itself to the core of your being.

Turning Touch Around

Shift your perceptions to touch. For example, take a stick or twig and hold it in your hand. Relax and be present with the experience of touch. Open yourself to it. Feel the presence of touch in the deepest level of yourself. Follow the sense of touch down below the place where you categorize it.

Feel down into yourself where touch is experienced absolutely, purely just like the clear mirror. Enjoy the experience of deep communion and the opening of Source through touch.

Turning Smell Around

This time, follow your sense of smell back to its origin. Allow the smells of Nature to penetrate deeper within you. Follow them back to where you experience the perception of those wonderful smells—back into the point of origination.

Turning Taste Around

If you have something in the outer world that you would like to taste, you can do the same practice with taste. You can taste a blade of grass or a bit of pinesap. Follow the taste back to Source.

Completing the Turning the Light Around Practice

For a few moments, just rest in the experience of inner clarity and spaciousness. Allow all the experiences of sight, sound, touch, smell, and taste to flow naturally back into you. It is almost as if you are at the center of a great medicine wheel or mandala where these senses radiate into the central core of your being. At the core of the sacred mandala is an absolutely pure, clear, spacious awareness that receives all these gifts of perception.

As you rest in this spontaneous appreciation of all the gifts from the wild, allow them to uncover that witnessing aspect of your deepest self, that part of your being that is pure witness of each sensory experience. Follow all of the perceptions back into that witness, back into that pure awareness. Enjoy the playful dance of inner nature dancing into the deepest essence of your inner witness. There is no need for effort. This happens spontaneously and naturally. Open into spacious awareness itself.

Next, allow the pure awareness to simply rest within this self-recognition. It is as if the deep inner witness is simply witnessing itself. Spacious clarity rests in itself, effortlessly, because it is your true nature. You really do not have to find it, because it is already there. All you have to do is to allow it to be.

I recommend that you do this practice in the morning and evening. By making this a daily pattern, you can continue going deeper into this natural opening. It is almost as if the shrouds that have obscured your true essence are being pulled away, and the light within begins to shine clearer and clearer. Ultimately one day, it will shine forth like a brilliant star in the vastness of space.

Resting in Source Practice #3: Sky Meditation

Sky meditation is an ancient practice from the Tibetan Dzogchen tradition. It is also found quite widely in both the Taoist and Native American traditions. This practice should be done in an open and spacious place, preferably where the sky is clear. So find a place where you can look directly into the sky without any obscurations like the Sun, trees, overhangs, or anything else that may distract you from the pure clarity and spaciousness of the sky. If you are fortunate enough to have a natural stone meditation seat, or a group of rocks that can help support you as you gaze out into the sky, that is quite auspicious.

In Nature, one of the closest, most intimate teachers of Source is the sky. By resting in a state of profound meditation with the sky, Father Sky can open you to a depth of realization of Source that no other aspect of Nature can.

- Initially, it is best to sit with your back straight and legs crossed, or in a standing meditation posture. If you are an experienced meditator, you can do this practice lying down or lying on an incline.

- Place your hands on the thighs with the palms in a receptive mode. Softly gaze into the sky so that you are seeing with your whole field of vision, without emphasizing center-pointed focus. The main objective for this meditation practice is clarity and spaciousness. So as you meditate, open your mind to those two aspects—the aspects of immense clarity and vast space. The clarity and spaciousness of the sky help inspire the realization of an even greater clarity and vastness that lies within you, which is the true, clear essence of Source.

- If there are a few clouds in the sky, relax and place your main attention on the emptiness of the sky. Just let the clouds, birds, or any other beings that are soaring in the sky come and go. Remain with your attention clearly focused on the sky itself. Let your eyes move into the sky's vastness. Bring your awareness into your eyes, and then let your eyes soar out into space. Soar out into the unbounded vastness. Let your mind merge with the clear and spacious aspect of the open sky. Let this practice inspire a sense of the sky-like awareness that resides within you. Let the mind rest in the space and the clear aspect of the sky. Focus on the clarity aspect of your mirrorlike awareness, not on the reflections.

- If you see any little lights or small nodules dancing in space, like a granular series of little rainbow colors, just let that happen. Bring your consciousness and your awareness back to the clarity of the space. If there are any floaters that pass through the sky, just let them come and go like a cloud. Continually bring your awareness back to a sky-like presence.

- After having dissolved into the outer sky, bring your awareness back inside. Let the sky pour back into you. Feel the immensity of all that clear space pouring back into you. Feel it connecting with your pure and spacious witness within. Let that vast, wild and free sky open the inner wildness. As the inner wildness opens, feel it opening even larger than the great vastness of the outer sky. The inner sky dawns as clear, free, unbounded, open inner space.

- Sense the natural inner connectedness between the outer sky and the inner sky. Enjoy the inspiration of how outer sky and inner sky penetrate each other. Let all thoughts, feelings, emotions, and perceptions just naturally appear and dissolve in the space and clarity.

- Then notice that while outer and inner sky open in union, an even vaster sky opens—a more secret one, the deepest level of your true being. This ultimate sky holds all form, births all form, and receives all form back into it without a trace, just like a finger writing in water. Rest in that vastness. Relax into that clarity. Dissolve into that spaciousness and open into that unbounded luminosity for as long as possible.

- Very gently bring yourself back into a normal state of consciousness. Recognize that the sky-like awareness is the foundation of all states of being, including your ordinary states. The inner sky-like witness continues to support and sustain you throughout the activities of the day and evening. Continue in a state of recognition of this pure unbounded sky-like awareness within for as long as you can. Move in that pure and unbounded state, no matter what is flowing through your life. Allow that state to remain as your fundamental truth throughout the day and night.

Spiritual Warriorship

YOU HAVE HAD A WONDERFUL JOURNEY IN Nature with this book as your companion. Hopefully, many aspects of these teachings have touched you. My greatest wish for you is that as your exploration strengthens, the healing power of Nature will continue to work its magic. May your journey deepen each time you apply the twelve principles for natural liberation, the six core principles, and the ways of cultivation we have learned here.

As your formal cultivation amplifies, how can you extend the insight, beauty, and peacefulness you receive? How can you bring this harmony into your everyday life? The practice of spiritual warriorship bridges the gap between your spiritual cultivation with these six principles and their application in your everyday life.

Ideally, you should try to spend an hour or two each day in a natural place that you find personally inspiring, cultivating the principles and supportive methods you have learned here. This practice will allow them to continue growing until they become part of you. Early morning, around the time of sunrise, is an excel-

lent time for formal cultivation—particularly for practices emphasizing clear, spacious meditation and energy development for
renewing life force. Another good time for practice is in the late
afternoon and at sunset. This is a fine time for those practices that
release the tensions and blockages of the day, and for deep relaxation. Whatever times you choose, make these cultivation times
the high points of your day; but do not restrict your practice solely
to these formal sessions. As you return to your everyday environment—at home, at work, in social situations—wherever possible,
spontaneously utilize the principles and practices you have
learned. Apply them dynamically in the flow of your daily life. For
many of my students who lead very busy lives, I recommend that
they set aside one or two hours a day when they continue with life
as usual—but they put their primary emphasis on spontaneously
applying one of the twelve principles to whatever is going on for
them at that time. The great majority of those who do this report
back that this is one of the most powerful practices of their life.

This approach works very well for Americans, who suffer
under the illusion that they never have enough time to practice—
to meditate, do Qi Gong, perform Yoga, and undertake other formal methods. For them this approach is the ultimate solution. No
time is lost, because one applies the principle they are working on
dynamically in the flow of everyday life. The only requirement is
to remember the hour you are committed to integrating the chosen
principle with your life—and doing it.

For those who are forgetful, skillful use of a watch with a
reminding buzzer can help. It is up to you to decide which principle to start with and when to shift to a new one. In general, I recommend starting with the first principle and then working on
through to the last over at least several months of daily practice. I
also find having two hour-long sessions per day works far more
powerfully than a single session. For example, you might choose
to do one hour in the morning and a second hour in the afternoon
or evening. Over time, it is a good idea to shift the time of the day

around for the hours you choose. This change allows you to learn how to spontaneously apply the principles in different situations. You might develop great skill in relaxing during the drive to work, but find you need more attention to learning how to relax during the hour of the daily staff meeting, for example. Once you feel complete with the full series of principles, then perhaps you can go back to a principle that you feel needs more attention, and work with that for a while; you might even want to work with it for differing hours on differing days. Or go back to the first principle again and carry the process deeper with your second round. You might begin with the six core principles emphasized in this book, and then go back later to work through the more comprehensive twelve principles for natural liberation series that I outlined in the first chapter of this book.

To illustrate how this spontaneous application of a principle might be done, let's take a look at the relaxation principle. In your flow through your normal daily life, each time you realize you are tense, practice relaxation. Pause for a moment. Take a deep breath into the tension. Recall the deep relaxation principle and practices you have worked with in this book. Recollect the sequence of relaxation: from first discovering where you hold tension; to learning how to decontract that stress; then actually mastering relaxation; next opening a new habitual path of relaxing into life; ultimately then opening the last great doorway, trust; to finally passing through the great threshold, surrender. Remember how it felt to be totally relaxed in the wild, and ask Nature to assist you. Allow your body to remember and return to that state spontaneously in the now. Should you forget to relax and become tense again during your hour of spontaneous application, don't beat yourself up for forgetting—that is simply another form of getting lost in tension and contraction. Instead, gently bring your awareness back again to the relaxation process and continue.

Remember, too, that energy follows thought. Visualize the energy of relaxation washing over you as you talk to a difficult customer, obstinate client, tough boss, or stressed employee. Once you are truly relaxed, you can be totally undistracted and present with them. This relaxed, liberated energy can potentially engender a spiritually transforming experience for you, for them, or—best of all—for both of you.

Tonglen is another practice that lends itself well to spontaneous expression. When you witness suffering, open your heart and breathe it in. Allow natural happiness to arise from the bottomless well of Source; feel it radiate out with each exhalation, liberating the suffering of all living beings around you. Where appropriate, teach these practices to others so that they can join in and also help other suffering beings. Merge your Tonglen with some form of concrete activity to help those in need. If people are starving, bring them food; if the forests are being destroyed, help plant new native trees; if a plant or animal is suffering from the threat of extinction, work to save its home and support its renewal.

The more you practice these spiritual processes, the more natural they become. They also provide a model for others in your community to support healing relationships among people and with Nature everywhere. The healing revitalization of the Earth and all its living beings truly begins only when we heal ourselves and renew our present relationships. Healing ourselves helps heal all our relations with all of life. Likewise, serving to heal all our relations helps heal ourselves.

The remaining emphasis in this final chapter is on becoming a spiritual warrior in the service of Mother Earth. As is stressed above, compassionate service is the heart of liberating action. As is also stressed in this book, the Earth is our common human temple and church, and the support for many enlightening processes explored here. Unfortunately, as most of us realize, the Earth is suffering an unrelenting degradation of her living systems at every level. Species are becoming extinct on a daily basis, and whole ecosystems are disappearing under the onslaught of human activity. Now even the entire planet is enduring the impacts of global climate change primarily induced by human use and greed for fossil fuels. In addition to global climate change, a saddening array of multiple global ecosystem impacts is accelerating—from tropical deforestation to serious oceanic pollution. And we do not have a clue what the combined impact will be of all these changes taken together—the synergistic factor. During most attempts to model global systems, this synergistic factor leads to an immense amplification of the negative impacts—far more than one might expect from simply adding up the impacts one by one. In effect, we are all conducting an unthinkably vast experiment that is determining the future of Gaia—without having an inkling of how the experiment truly will turn out. All that can be said now is that the best science points to profoundly ominous changes for all life, unless we humans can change our ways. Those of us who have knowingly received so much from Mother Earth should be at the forefront of efforts to transform this global onslaught.

Most of the suggestions covered in the following text are suggestions for activity. They are not meant to be a comprehensive review of what needs to be done; rather, they are meant to stimulate your own creativity born out of a profound love of Gaia. For those of you who have been blessed with the opportunity to do a Sacred Passage or a vision quest, you know what I mean. You have received what I often refer to as "the Earth empowerment." Many, many others of you have received this same empowerment through ways of communion that lead to the same reunion: Mother Gaia's beingness now flows in your spirit's neural veins. You become one with her as a vehicle to help transform humankind into harmonious brothers and sisters of all species.

As you engage in the great work to help bring humanity back into global ecosystem balance and harmony, it is important to unify this outer process with the sacred principles and practices outlined in this book. This is the essence of spiritual warriorship. I strongly recommend you practice the application of all these principles in the midst of your work to transform our culture. If you do not do this, and instead become caught up in creating enemies and obstacles as the center point for your awareness, the sacred view is lost. The essence of spiritual warrior practice is to bring each principle into the very heart of your activity to shift humanity's presence within Gaia to a loving, sustaining communion. If you fall into seeing those intent upon destroying the Earth as only the enemy, then you fall into the same primal separation that is the deepest cause of their destructive behavior on Earth. Your challenge is to engage the process of transformation so that you can see your enemy as actually your teacher. Your enemies are there to teach you how to accomplish the realization with yourself that *all* forms arise from Source, manifest in Source, and dissolve back into Source, moment by moment. As the first of the twelve principles clearly states, all apparently separate forms are actually one, completely interconnected; yet they dance in apparent separation at the same time.

In your spiritual warriorship service for Mother Earth, you must ultimately learn to embrace your inner demons of fear and anger as they arise; your opponent helps bring these demons up for you to then transform. In transforming this fear and anger, energy and awareness are liberated — freed to be of far greater service in both inner and positive outer transformation than if you remained stuck and blocked, angrily fighting your enemy. So this is the challenge as you read through all of this chapter's recommendations for ways to serve Mother Gaia.

I recommend that you initially pick a range of spiritual warriorship activities that you feel you can handle; don't go so overboard with taking on service that you drown. To receive some deep answers on this I recommend doing a vision quest or Sacred Passage. During your solo, pose the question of how to be of highest service, and then let go and remain open, empty, and listening. Whatever answer arises, arises from a profound level. Having chosen your initial range of service, begin the work. The work is to take each principle (ideally from the twelve principles) at a time, and give yourself time to put the principle into practice. Initially, keep it simple and focus on one principle at a time—to be applied in the service for the Earth work that you have chosen. Over time, sequentially go through each of the twelve principles for natural liberation in this way. When complete with that cycle, you will have realized an extraordinary inner transformation through your spiritual warriorship.

For the most part, it will be easier to start working with one of the earlier principles first, and slowly move through each one of the remaining principles as you feel you are ready. In this way, each principle lays the foundation for grounded development of the next. For example, suppose you are working to help save the extraordinary pristine wilderness of the Arctic National Wildlife Refuge in northern Alaska from oil development. In your work, you feel anger and contractedness rising in you much of the time, because so little progress is being made to protect the refuge, and the economic, political, and media power of those who want to develop the area is huge. As you do your work, you consciously relax into your anger, sadness, tension, and contractedness. As you master this process, you start to feel all the blocked energy melt away, and you no longer feel paralyzed by the situation. In fact, you start to feel increasingly energized, with much more available energy to do your warriorship work. At some point, you feel ready to focus on the next principle, presence. Although you have suc-ceeded in freeing up much more energy through mastering relaxed unblocking, you still feel distractedness pulling at your mind; your ability to focus is deficient. Thoughts arise uncon-trolled, such as: What might happen if the wrong strategy is cho-sen? How might past issues that are unresolved affect the battle? Where could future actions destroy any hope of success? To this kind of mind, presence is applied spontaneously in the process of thinking about strategy and in your actions. In addition, you may want to support strengthening presence by some formal medita-tion practice to fortify one-pointed focus. Soon, your ability unfolds to stay clear, calm, relaxed, and focused on the process at hand. You find that your energy is much more powerful, because little is being dissipated in superfluous worries. As a spiritual warrior, your capacity has strengthened and more is being accomplished externally. Internally, the principles of relaxation and presence are grounding themselves at a far deeper level of your being.

Now let's look into a range of some of the activities of Earth service. Any of these can provide you with the ground for refining the inner principles of spiritual warriorship.

As you learn to walk lightly on the Earth, you may want to do something in your own community to bring awareness of how to cultivate Spirit in Nature or to help revitalize the Earth. There are many others around the world with the same or similar visions. Contact groups that have already formed, and work together to create a harmonious community and demonstrate a renewed relationship with all living beings. If you feel moved to do so, help form a local Way of Nature Fellowship group in your own area. Contact Sacred Passage and The Way of Nature to see about bringing in guides and teachers to help you begin deepening your group. Consider training to become a Sacred Passage or The Way of Nature guide for your region. Contact your schools to find ways to bring contact with Nature back into education. Work with schools to provide students with regular alone time in Nature, under well-protected circumstances. Promote bringing into our culture the ancient Native American practice of providing the vision quest as the rite of passage for people during their mid-teens.

Learn about your home bioregion. If there are possibilities to help protect a local natural area that has special sacred qualities, begin the process to protect it. Find others in your area of like spirit and work together. Research potential sources of support for preserving your natural, sacred land. Go to those sources and work to see them help protect and honor your community's sacred lands.

Contact the Sacred Land Trust *(www.sacredpassage.com)* for other ideas and assistance in knowing how you might proceed. Remember, the concept of preserving wild and natural land as sacred, as the temple or church, is still an alien idea to most non–Native Americans. This view of the Earth itself as sacred, and of certain special natural sites as particularly sacred, is one of the great gifts to us all from our Native American brothers and sisters. We are way overdue in finding and protecting sacred places as natural places of worship, provided directly by Great Spirit and Gaia. A beginning model for this is the Sacred Land Trust in Crestone, Colorado; those helping create this model are doing so in the hope that Crestone's Sacred Land Trust can help give birth to thousands of similar initiatives elsewhere—and to reverse the Western antipathy toward experiencing the sacred in Nature. Clearly, if we are to have an Earth with humans in balance with all of life, we must have an Earth-centered spirituality and natural sacred places to meditate and worship outside of human-built structures. Become involved with the effort to help our culture and its various religions to move in this direction of an Earth-centered spirituality.

Begin looking at your home, your neighborhood, your town, your county, your watershed, your airshed, and your state as natural systems. Discover how the Earth supports healthy ecosystems at all these levels. Learn how matter and energy cycle through these systems and how many different species support each other to benefit all life in an overall balanced and harmonious way. Study Nature and its incredibly diverse, interwoven ecosystems. Study your own body and see how intricately it unfolds as part of Nature's natural systems. Learn how Nature tries to recycle everything. Discover how Gaia can take all organic decay and wastes and turn them into fertilizer and soil for new growth. Explore how Nature maintains living systems that distribute solar-captured energy out through an extraordinary array of living communities and organisms, including you. Meditate and contemplate on how to redesign our homes, towns, farms, and human systems so that they function as healthy organs within the vaster ecosystems that support them. Find out what ecologically sustainable technologies, such as solar and wind power, are available and practical where you live. Do you know what is produced locally in the way of food, clothing, water, and fuel? What must be imported? Where does it come from? How much regional capital is lost to the regional economy by exporting it elsewhere to purchase distant goods? How stable is the economy in your area? What are your dependencies on other regions, and how are their goods trans-ported to you? What opportunities exist to accelerate the recycling of capital within your bioregion? What do you need to do or learn to be able to live more simply, in a way that is more sustainably connected to Gaia? Start where you are and cultivate a deeper, more ecologically harmonious relationship with your home, your community, and your local ecoregion. Share your insights with others. As a true spiritual warrior, help shift our culture's field toward a more balanced, harmonious relationship with all life. That is one of the most important things any of us can do.

Listed below are a few ways you can begin making these cru-cial connections. However, don't limit yourself to these few ideas. When you meditate in Nature, do an eleven direction ceremony or rainbow light visualization; ask Great Spirit and Mother Earth for guidance, for insight, for the means to help us and our culture transform. Go out on a vision quest to pray; do ceremony and meditate to receive true vision on how to help our troubled Western culture. Enter a Sacred Passage to commune deeply with Nature and to touch Source; out of that profound communion can come a creativity that is beyond predictions. You may receive answers to questions we have not even learned to ask.

- Plant organically grown vegetables, flowers, and trees. Local nurseries will be able to advise you on selection and care. If you do not grow your own vegetables, find out where you can buy organic food produced in your own area (these are not only healthier for your body; your support will help strengthen the local bioregional economy on which your own livelihood depends).

- Universities, colleges, and local food coops often sponsor agricultural extension programs. If there is one in your area, use it to get tips on natural pest and weed controls for your garden and trees. (You will also find information at your public library and on the Internet.)

- Many organic farmers now offer subscription programs in which you pay a fixed amount for the growing season and share the crops with other subscribers. This is a good way to eat more healthily while supporting Earth-friendly farming practices.

- Call the county water department and ask where your water comes from. Buy a map of your region and explore the details of your home watershed. Hike to follow the small rivulets down to the larger streams and rivers. Discover what other kinds of life share the watershed with you. Start spending sacred time in your watershed's natural areas and begin bonding more deeply with local plants, animals, birds, and elements of Nature. Find out where local streams feed into your home reservoir. Trace the path of the water from its reservoir to your faucet. Learn where the water treatment plant is, and find out what chemicals are added to the water you use. Uncover all the potential sources of pollution there are from local factories, home developments, and agrochemical pollution. Discover local natural springs with good water and gather your drinking water from there in glass jugs. Become involved with local water pollution issues and with efforts to clean up your area's streams and rivers.

Organize your community to work together with you. Help with the organic renewal of your waterways in any way you can.

- Call your local The Nature Conservancy, Sierra Club, Greenpeace, Natural Resources Defense Council, World Wildlife Fund, Friends of the Earth, The Wilderness Society, The Way of Nature Fellowship, Sacred Land Trust, or other environmental protection group to find out what activities you might want to participate in. Donate some of your time and energy to the protection of designated natural areas, parks, wildlife refuges, wild rivers, and wilderness areas. Find out how you can help support the permanent protection of what major wilderness and roadless areas still exist. Give particular attention to those areas of great national or international significance, as well as to unique local natural and wild areas where your vote can make all the difference. Regularly call, telegram, write, or email your state and national representatives and senators on these issues. If possible, make personal appointments to see your political representatives in person to push for these wilderness issues. Organize for change with all those you know of like mind and communicate with your representatives as whole blocks of people. Remember, once wild and natural places are destroyed, they are effectively gone forever. Once a species becomes extinct, all of us and Gaia are permanently poorer.

- Volunteer to spend time scouting out natural areas and sacred sites within your bioregion. Develop strategies for their preservation and wise use. Conduct group ceremony, prayer, and meditation circles in Nature to ask for the good heart and wisdom to provide what Mother Earth needs.

• Contact your local chamber of commerce and ask what the major manufacturing industries are in your area. Ask for information on pollution issues and what is being done to resolve these problems. Get involved with innovative solutions to pollution control that support the development of new, natural ecosystem-sustaining technologies and companies. Read the business news to learn how your local economy works. When you go out to eat, ask the restaurateur where he or she gets the food you are eating. Ask for organically grown food free from pesticides, synthetic chemical fertilizers, and genetic modification. Educate your local community on these issues.

• Investigate what corporations, banks, and mutual funds support only green businesses and those that are socially responsible. Shift your retirement and saving investments into such companies and urge your friends, associates, and people in your workplace to do the same. Similarly, pull your investments out of socially irresponsible and environmentally destructive and unsustainable companies. Be vocal in local media about why you are doing this and advocate others to do the same. Urge your friends, broader community, local businesses, colleges, universities, and retirement funds to shift all their portfolios into socially and environmentally sustainable investments.

• Become active in local and state educational organizations, and encourage education, research, and new technology creation in areas that will lead to ecologically sustainable development. Emphasize that the conversion of an inefficient, environmentally destructive cultural system into a culture that is in harmony with natural systems will take an enormous shift in research, development, market creation, and overall application. The good news is that this shift into an environmentally sustainable culture will provide a massive new infusion of technology creation, opening markets, job creation, and new capital. To pull it off, the economic effort is not unlike the shift of emphasis required when a nation goes to war. With war, there may be economic infusions into the companies making war technology—but the cost in suffering is immense. By contrast, the shift to becoming a truly harmonious ecological culture would provide large and numerous positive side effects throughout the culture and economy. If such an emphasis can be created, it will come at a time when Western culture needs just such a new vision to avoid economic and social stagnation.

- Watch your local newspapers for news of Gaia-friendly activities. These activities may include initiatives to protect endangered species, cleanups of local waterways, recycling drives, efforts to reduce crop spraying or industrial pollution, herb walks, community carpooling, bike-to-work days, fund-raising activities for environmental groups, environmental education. . . . the more you explore, the more you will discover possibilities for honing your awareness of the Earth and her diverse voices. As the bumper sticker suggests, "Think Globally; Act Locally." Everything you do to heal your local ecosystem is an important step toward healing the Earth.

- Ask your employer to subsidize bus passes or to offer incentives for carpooling or bicycling. Support building walking and biking trails in both suburbs and cities. Look into ways for our culture to help reinvigorate mass transit and railroad transportation to reduce dependency on single-passenger vehicles. Purchase electric, hybrid, and biodiesel cars, and push society for accelerated conversion to these same systems. Start recycling programs where you work and where you live, or research the possibility of expanding an existing one.

- Join a group or club that celebrates Nature in your area. Depending on where you live, there will probably be groups devoted to camping, cycling, mountain climbing, kayaking, canoeing, bird watching, hiking, cross-country skiing, scuba diving and snorkeling, and outdoor and nature photography. Take advantage of these opportunities to learn from people who know the local terrain, and to enjoy the community of others who love the wild.

- Become a bird watcher. Learn to recognize the songs of all of the birds in your area. Spend some time learning the plants and animals of your home ecosystem. Go into Nature and become friends with these fellow travelers. Spend time alone and quiet in natural places to deepen your communion with neighborhood plants, animals, and birds. Discover which plants and herbs are helping healers for maintaining good health or for healing specific illnesses. Enroll in tracking courses to learn to read the language of Nature.

- Study with Bach and local flower essence practitioners to learn the vibrational and healing powers of flower essences. Work with the essences to clarify your mental, emotional, and energy bodies. Discover how these essences link you powerfully to Nature, particularly through flowering plants from your home ecosystem. Learn to dowse and practice selecting flower essences that are helpful for yourself and others. Last, become skilled at making local flower essences from the flowers themselves. With like-minded friends, explore the effects of using these essences for healing and spiritual growth.

- Research the Native American tribes that once populated your state. What were their principal foods? How did they travel? What natural features, crops, or substances did they use in their rituals? What insights did they have about living in harmony with your local bioregion? How might you apply these same insights to helping our own culture transform into more harmonious relationships with the Earth? Since the original human occupants of your region were not dependent on massive materials imports, fossil fuels, or a global economy, their lifestyles and customs can reveal much about ecologically sustainable ways of living compatibly with Nature in the same ecosystem you inhabit.

- Investigate replacing the utilities you currently use with alternative, renewable power sources, such as wind, water (particularly mini-hydro), or solar power. Mobilize your neighborhood, broader community, county, and local cities to adopt strong energy conservation measures and to replace fossil fuel and nuclear plants with ecologically sustainable, renewable energy systems. Like all energy procedures, renewables require a capital investment; however, in most situations these energy sources can easily pay for themselves and actually save you and your local community considerable money. This is particularly true when conversion happens with whole neighborhoods and communities. By reducing dependence on foreign oil, renewable energy promotes homeland security and removes the motivation to interfere in the affairs of oil-rich countries. Utilization of renewable energy sources also prevents precious capital from being exported outside your home bioregion, and encourages capital recycling within your local community. Because most renewable energy sources are inherently decentralized (such as collection of wind, mini-hydro, and solar electric), they make a great contribution to national security because no single act of war or terror can knock out the system. Highly centralized systems such as big coal and oil plants or nuclear power plants are relatively easy to get at and destroy; therefore, shifting into highly decentralized, renewable energy systems provides a great boost to national and homeland security. Also, renewable energy systems are naturally harmonized with most living ecosystems and cause little or no pollution. Their use also contributes dramatically to reducing fossil fuel use, and therefore to reducing global warming.

- Join together in groups and circles to meditate and pray for the healing of the Earth, each other, and all the species we share this extraordinary planet with. Do this on a regular—at least weekly—basis. Work together with the practices in this book, such as the rainbow light meditation, Tonglen, and the eleven directions ceremony. Working with others, develop Great Spirit– and Earth-centered group meditations, visualizations, prayers, and ceremonies. Practice them together in Nature. Give some attention to group visualization practice to see pollution of every kind transmuted and transformed. There is growing evidence that group practice like this can heal, and even reverse, forms of planetary contamination and degradation. Lend your life force to the healing of the Earth and all her life species with these meditations and visualizations. Such practice also should inspire you to follow up with some of the concrete actions described earlier.

These are only initial suggestions. There are literally countless ways you can tend to the Earth while simultaneously cultivating your own relationship with the natural world and deepening your cultivation of the twelve principles of natural liberation. As you engage in these environmental transformations, carry the essence of spiritual warriorship with you. No matter what the challenge, remain relaxed, be present, and radiate an open heart. Return to your original nature. Rest in Source.

Concluding
Thoughts

I WOULD LIKE TO LEAVE YOU WITH just a few thoughts. For all of us, life is very short. None of us knows when these forms we call ourselves will end. I hope the practices and the principles I have shared throughout this book will greatly enrich your life—however many years you remain in Mother Gaia's embrace. Since you have now received these principles of liberation and some methods that support their unfolding, why not take them to heart? Each principle contains a liberating seed within. When you embrace the practices that help these seeds to sprout, a potent process of liberation is germinated. Spending time alone in Nature fertilizes this growth. Natural meditation, energy development, ceremony, and prayer water the burgeoning tree of life.

These ways of cultivation allow you to move very deeply into joyful, real essence. So spend as much time as possible cultivating inner truth in Nature. The uncontrived nature of wilderness supports communion with the naked essence of ourselves. Just regularly *being* in Nature can bring joy and happiness. As the artifices of culture fall away, our original face can be glimpsed. This glimpse can enrich your life in ways that are beyond imagination. The vision quest can crack the seed coat that prevents inner freedom from blossoming. Half an hour, an hour, or an occasional weekend spent in communion with Nature and Spirit, merging inner and outer nature, can be the foundation for an extraordinarily rich, full existence. In my own life, Nature and Great Spirit have been the most reliable and steady spiritual supports. They have been my church and temple, phenomenal teachers, great friends, wonderful lovers, and faithful companions on the journey of life.

Existence is unpredictable—an unpredictable miracle. Wilderness reflects the magic, majesty, and unpredictable creativity of the universe and Spirit. If you totally embrace Nature, and "the Great Spirit that moves through all things," your life will be full, enriched, and realized beyond measure.

Realize the Great Mystery dances within and through you. Open to the vastness and radiance that is your true birthright. Rest in the free and open natural state. Remain in Source.

About the Author

JOHN P. MILTON is a frequent lecturer and workshop leader, and a pioneering, renowned, and sought-after meditation and Qi Gong teacher. Thousands of people have sought his instruction since he began teaching in the 1950's.

He has developed unique practices for uniting inner and outer nature through training in Buddhist, Taoist, Vedantic, Tantric, and Native American traditions, and he incorporates T'ai Chi and yoga in his work.

Milton is also known for organizing and leading dozens of expeditions into some of the wildest areas left on Earth, starting in his late teens. He received his M.S. in ecology and conservation from the University of Michigan in 1963. A founding father of the environmental movement in the early 1960's, he was a professor of environmental studies and a Woodrow Wilson Center scholar at the Smithsonian Institute. He was one of the first ecologists on staff at the White House as a member of the President's Council of Economic Advisors, and was a founding member of the environmental organization Friends of the Earth.

Milton was instrumental in introducing the vision quest to contemporary culture. In 1945, at the time he began his sacred solo retreats in the wilderness, vision quests were unknown in the Americas outside Native American culture.

For years, this author has written books and articles on inner development and ecology. He founded Threshold, a foundation devoted to spiritual liberation in nature. His programs inspire Earth stewardship by cultivating natural wisdom and an open, loving heart in the wild.

For more information about John P. Milton and his teachings and programs, as well as his publications and audiovisual materials, or for more information on The Way of Nature, including its regional and international groups, contact:

Sacred Passage & The Way of Nature Fellowship
P.O. Box 3388
Tucson, AZ 85722
(877) 818-1881
info@sacredpassage.com
www.sacredpassage.com

To order John's tape set *Sky Above, Earth Below,* which was the original basis for this book, contact: *www.soundstrue.com.*

Sentient Publications, LLC publishes books on cultural creativity, experimental education, transformative spirituality, holistic health, new science, ecology, and other topics, approached from an integral viewpoint. Our authors are intensely interested in exploring the nature of life from fresh perspectives, addressing life's great questions, and fostering the full expression of the human potential. Sentient Publications' books arise from the spirit of inquiry and the richness of the inherent dialogue between writer and reader.

We are very interested in hearing from our readers. To direct suggestions or comments to us, or to be added to our mailing list, please contact:

SENTIENT PUBLICATIONS, LLC
1113 Spruce Street
Boulder, CO 80302
303-443-2188
contact@sentientpublications.com
www.sentientpublications.com